Using Intensive Interaction and Sensory Integration

by the same author

From Isolation to Intimacy
Making Friends without Words
Phoebe Caldwell with Jane Horwood
ISBN 978 1 84310 500 8

Finding You Finding Me
Using Intensive Interaction to get in touch with people whose severe learning disabilities are combined with autistic spectrum disorder
ISBN 978 1 84310 399 8

of related interest

Promoting Social Interaction for Individuals with Communicative Impairments
Making Contact
Edited by M. Suzanne Zeedyk
ISBN 978 1 84310 539 8

Understanding Sensory Dysfunction
Learning, Development and Sensory Dysfunction in Autism Spectrum Disorders, ADHD, Learning Disabilities and Bipolar Disorder
Polly Godwin Emmons and Liz McKendry Anderson
ISBN 978 1 84310 806 1

Sensory Perceptual Issues in Autism and Asperger Syndrome
Different Sensory Experiences – Different Perceptual Worlds
Olga Bogdashina
Forewords by Wendy Lawson and Theo Peeters
ISBN 978 1 84310 166 6

Autism – The Eighth Colour of the Rainbow
Learn to Speak Autistic
Florica Stone
ISBN 978 1 84310 182 6

Using Intensive Interaction and Sensory Integration

A Handbook for Those who Support People with Severe Autistic Spectrum Disorder

Phoebe Caldwell
with Jane Horwood

Jessica Kingsley Publishers
London and Philadelphia

First published in 2008
by Jessica Kingsley Publishers
116 Pentonville Road
London N1 9JB, UK
and
400 Market Street, Suite 400
Philadelphia, PA 19106, USA

www.jkp.com

Library of Congress Cataloging in Publication Data
A CIP catalog record for this book is available from the Library of Congress

British Library Cataloguing in Publication Data
A CIP catalogue record for this book is available from the British Library

ISBN 978 1 84310 626 5

Printed and bound in Great Britain by
MPG Books Group, Cornwall

Contents

1

Introduction

There is now a great surge of interest in autism. Many books are being written (those written by people with autism are particularly useful) and films being made. Most of these are about children who are on the more able end of the autistic spectrum. What this handbook offers is a simple and practical way of getting close to those children and adults with very severe autism, some who also have severe learning disability, many of whom do not speak and some of whom are showing serious or extreme behavioural distress. We feel as cut off from them as they are from us.

Throughout this handbook, we shall refer to the child or adult with whom we are working as our *communication partner* or simply *partner*. *Intensive Interaction* uses body language to communicate with children and adults in a way that establishes attention and emotional engagement. *Sensory Integration* uses physical sensations to focus attention. The reason for combining these two approaches in a single handbook is that when put together they provide an extremely powerful structure to help the confused brain of an autistic child or adult know what they are doing. In a world that appears frightening and chaotic, what the approaches have in common is that both put in place signals that the brain can recognise and on which it can focus. In a situation where, for example, Thérèse Jolliffe (who is autistic) tells us that she lives in terror and spends her whole life trying to work out what is happening, we are trying to construct a map that has meaning for our partner.

As practitioners, both authors have benefited from what they have learned from each other. For example, Jane finds that when she uses Intensive Interaction to tune in to the rhythm of a child's movements, she can get through to her much more quickly than would otherwise be the case. On the other hand, Phoebe finds that there are times when using the techniques of Sensory Integration in parallel with body language helps her partner to know what they are doing and where they are in space.

This handbook is selective. It does not address the question of diets, nor does it compare all the different educational systems such as the PECS (Picture Exchange Communication System) and TEACCH (Treatment and Education of Autistic and related Communica-tion-handicapped CHildren) that are used to try and teach people on the autistic spectrum to deal with the world they live in. On the subject of the intestinal symptoms that a proportion of people on the autistic spectrum experience, we take the view that, as is the case for those who are not on the spectrum, medical problems require medical solutions.

However, since we cannot teach anyone anything if they are not listening to us, in this handbook we shall be focusing on getting our autistic partner's attention, in a way that their brain finds non-invasive and intriguing. By providing an environment that is user-friendly, Intensive Interaction lays the ground for further, more strictly educa-tional approaches. It does not claim to be a cure for autism. Its effect is in establishing emotional communication. It does not cost anyone anything. Many parents and support staff working with adults who use Intensive Interaction say such things as 'My daughter is happy now'. Her brain is able to make sense of what is going on round her without getting snarled up in a faulty processing system.

COMMUNICATION WITH PEOPLE WITH SEVERE AUTISM

First of all we need to think about what we mean when we talk about communication. Communication is about our ability to share our lives with other people.

We are born with the need to do this since we shall not survive if we cannot communicate our need for warmth, food, shelter, etc. From birth we cannot live independently; we need a mother or mother figure who will nurture us and with whom we can engage. As we grow older, however much we strive for independence, we are dependent on the society in which we live. We feel estranged from those with whom we cannot communicate and make strenuous efforts to learn a mutual language. And if our children cannot speak, we devise symbol and sign systems to bridge the gap that we feel exists between us and those to whom we cannot talk. But despite our best efforts, there are some people on the autistic spectrum who still seem to be beyond our reach. They have little or no meaningful speech. They do not respond to our approaches or only to a very limited extent. So what can we possibly mean when we talk about having a conversation with children and adults who are not only non-verbal but also seem to reject our attempts to get in touch and even reject us as people? To be treated with the casualness with which one might treat a piece of furniture reduces us to an object and we feel alienated.

If we are going to discuss communication, it helps if we think about the nature of the way that we, neurotypical people, communicate with each other. What sort of conversations do we have with each other?

Figure 1.1 Want a cup of tea?

Functional communication

First of all there is *functional communication*, through which we make
our needs known to each other and convey information. We greet each
other. We talk to each other. We negotiate and we discuss things that
interest us.

Note that functional communication need not be verbal; it is also
served by communication systems such as PECS and sign systems. If
our partner is on the spectrum, then the less able they are, the more
concrete the system we use needs to be. The more abstract a communication system is, the more difficult it will be for our partner to make
sense of it, since it will involve interpretation and so suffer from at least
some of the same disadvantages as speech, in that it will also involve
faulty processing, one of the underlying roots of stress in people on the
autistic spectrum. In practice I find that, when working with less able
people on the spectrum, the most effective interventions, those that
aim to establish a need, use simple *gesture* and also *objects of reference*.
Objects of reference are objects which are directly linked to an activity,
for example a towel refers to 'bath'. Even some of our more able
partners may find these supplements helpful. For example, objects
which have weight and texture can be a clearer mode for conveying
information than vision for some partners since they can continue to

'feel' the communication during the event. They can hang on to it; it does not so easily slip out of the brain's conscious grasp.

The problem is that if we focus exclusively on functional communication, there is the danger that we direct our partner's attention towards manipulating the world rather than helping them to share it. Even if we help them express 'happy' and 'sad' by choosing a face that expresses that feeling, it is distanced, it is not something that we share together. Better than nothing, it remains an observation rather than a mutual experience, communication fact rather than flow. It does not help us to feel in tune with each other.

So what other sorts of conversation can we expect?

Emotional engagement

Critically, emotional engagement lets us know how we feel about each other. However, it is an aspect of communication that is commonly thought to be missing in our interactions with our autistic partners.

Figure 1.2 'Aaaah!'

While both functional communication and emotional engagement are clearly desirable, when we look at Figures 1.1 and 1.2 – 'Want a cup of tea?' and 'Aaaahh!' – the difference between them is obvious. It can be summed up in a single word: *relationship*. Emotional engagement addresses the fundamental human need to connect and belong. Donna Williams, who has autism, describes her aloneness when she talks about how 'she had all her relationships which she should have had out there, with the shadow people in her inner world'.[1] However much we fulfil our partner's physical needs they will continue to feel isolated – 'an alien in a foreign land' – unless we can find a way of helping them to experience human bonding. We see a change in our partners when they begin to enjoy human company. They start to smile, look at us, refer back to us and seek our company.

How can we bring about this transformation?

USING BODY LANGUAGE

Intensive Interaction is the name given to an approach that uses body language to communicate and its aim is to establish emotional engagement. Although we may not be aware of it, we are doing this all the time. We are scanning, not just what our partners say but how they are saying it, what their facial expression and posture are telling us – and simply the way they are saying it, the tone, pitch, speed and rhythm of their speech. What does this tell us about how they are feeling? For example, does what they are saying and what they are expressing through their facial language tell the same story? We find ourselves uneasy if they do not – 'Something, I can't quite put my finger on it, doesn't add up.'

We all use facial expression and hand movements to supplement our communications. Do we make these in a calm or agitated manner? For example, the same hand movement may be welcoming or threatening. We use our perception of *how* it is done to decode how our partner feels – and we use our own body language to let them know

---

1   Williams (1995).

how we feel, even if we are not aware of what we are doing at the time. How we do respond will convey how we feel. In fact body language is the voice of *affect* (how we feel). It is through reading our partner's body language and responding with our own that we come to emotional understanding. In a negative sense, the classic example of contradiction is of a person who folds their arms across their chest, frowns and says through gritted teeth, 'I'm perfectly all right, thank you.' Their body language is contradicting the sense of what they are saying. We could say the 'vibes' are all wrong.

Body language helps us to tune in to each other's affective state; how they feel. The extent to which we are able to be sensitive to how others feel will allow us to build emotional engagement and trust.

There is some suggestion that up to 80 per cent of what we communicate with each other is through exchange of body language, rather than through exchange of verbal information. The use of Intensive Interaction is going to focus our attention on this aspect of exchange: not only what our partner is doing but also how they are doing it.

Two processes underpin Intensive Interaction and settle it in its place in communication. The first is the infant–mother paradigm, the first communicative interactions between mother and baby. Even at 20 minutes' old, the baby will copy its mother if she sticks out her tongue. Mother and baby are talking to each other from the moment of birth.

If the infant says, 'Boo', the mother will answer, 'Boo'. When she has sufficiently confirmed the infant sound (or movement) the baby tries out something else, say, 'Da'. The pattern that emerges is that when the baby initiates, the mother confirms and the baby is able to move on. The mother's confirmation of the baby's sound or movement appears to act as a release mechanism. This process remains hidden in our psyche all our lives and as adults we may be surprised to find, for example, that if we get stuck in anger, we are released only when an outside 'mother figure' confirms our distress. (As we discuss in the section on speech in Chapter 7, sometimes a 'hiccup' develops, where the grown child fails to achieve independence from the mother figure and is unable to proceed from intention to action until confirmed by the mother figure or substitute.)

The second process underlying Intensive Interaction relates to the operation of a network of nerve cells in the brain known as the *mirror neuron system*. It is the mirror neuron system that allows us to recognise what another person is doing (and hence be able to copy their action).

Let us imagine that John is looking at Mary. Mary moves her hand. If we look at what is happening in Mary's brain through a scanner while she is making this movement, we see that her action is accompanied by the firing of a particular pattern of nerve cells. John is also under a scanner, so we can watch what happens when he sees Mary's movement. What is so extraordinary is that, as he looks at her activity, the same pathway fires in John's brain. Simply watching her, his own brain has reproduced an identical map of neuron activity to hers.

Even more fascinating is that this recognition works for emotions as well as for actions. If I see you looking sad, it may well evoke an empathetic wave of sadness in me (although whether or not I notice this depends on where my attention is focused; I may even recognise the feeling later on, acknowledging it to myself with the comment, 'Oh, I missed that').

One suggestion about autism is that the mirror neuron system is not working, which is why some people on the spectrum are said to have difficulty in actions such as copying hand movements – and, by extrapolation, understanding how other people are feeling. However, experiments designed to test this idea use actions that are not necessarily part of the person with autism's normal repertoire. Putting aside for the present that the problem for some people with autism is that they are over-sensitive to emotional feelings rather than under-sensitive, in practice, if you engage your partner through the activities that are part of their life experience and therefore are meaningful – things they would normally do – your partner will recognise them every time. We have to recognise and respond to these, rather than copy.

What we get is not a copying game but an ongoing and open-ended conversation that is recognised as such by both parties. Deep down, this way of communicating with each other remains with us as a process all our lives. If I see someone else doing something, it fires off the same network of mirror neurons in my brain as would be triggered if I was doing it myself. In a literal sense, I feel what you are doing. The mirror neurons in our brain recognise and latch on to this extremely quickly. Even if we have autism, clinical experience confirms that our mirror neuron system does recognise our partner's initiatives provided they are part of our normal repertoire.

And Intensive Interaction is a shared process: it is something we do together. Whether or not the autistic partner's mirror neurons are functioning normally, working through body language allows the non-autistic partner to pick up and share how the autistic partner is feeling, so we can tune in to their affective state. We can build empathy into our responses. Now we can interact not only with what each other is doing but also to how our partner is feeling. To go back to the infant–mother paradigm, we can confirm their feelings (and it is especially important to confirm their negative feelings as well as their positive ones, otherwise we undermine their sense of self; it is about how they actually feel, not how we feel they ought to feel).

Now we can share joy and sorrow, meeting the need so powerfully expressed by Thérèse Jolliffe when she writes that it is not true that people on the spectrum do not feel emotions. 'We do love people, we do feel lonely', she writes, but then goes on to say that it is difficult to handle the physical feedback that the expression of such emotions entails.[2] We have found a way of talking to each other that appears to bypass the processing system that is at the centre of autistic disturbances: a pathway that allows us to engage with each other. We can share how we feel without apparently triggering the negative effects that drive a person on the autistic spectrum back into their inner world.

Before we go any further, I should like to emphasise that Intensive Interaction, based as it is on a process that is a natural part of our development – one that we have all been through – is not difficult to practise. As a practitioner remarked, 'In fact you do not even have to be frightfully good at it to get at least some change.' Although we may

---

2   Jolliffe, Lansdown and Robinson (1992).

start with 'imitation', what develops is a flexible interchange that builds into a conversation out of the language with which our partner is familiar, using the elements of their body language instead of words.

Intensive Interaction works right across the spectrum of non-verbal people (and with some who are verbal) (see Chapter 7). So what exactly are the special problems associated with using it with people on the autistic spectrum? Why do we feel especially cut off from them and do we need to do more than just use body language to communicate with them? For example, if I wear a brightly patterned jersey, all my attempts to engage the attention of my partner may be drowned in the visual confusion that I am triggering. So do we need to do more than just use body language to communicate with them?

THE AUTISM-FRIENDLY ENVIRONMENT

At any one time, our brains are taking in and processing millions of bits of information, teasing out the items that are important, putting these in context and writing the story of our lives as we live it, trying to make sense of what is going on.

The problem for people with autism is that although their sensory organs, the eyes, ears and touch sensors, may be working perfectly and feeding in the correct signals, the processing system, the ability to sift and isolate one thing, to relate it to another and to put it in context, may, at best, be working intermittently: in some people at the extreme end of the autistic spectrum, it may not be working at all. They live in a chaotic soup of unprocessed stimuli, a condition that is not only confusing and stressful but can also be terrifying and painful. They may feel that their only option is to withdraw into a world of their own making, focusing on a particular stimulus to the exclusion of those that so disturb them. We say they are 'switched off', that they are 'in a world of their own', and we feel totally unable to connect with them.

The aim of this handbook is to show that when we understand the terms of this condition and offer an *autism-friendly* environment (one that has the effect of reducing the stress with which the brain is struggling), the autistic person's brain relaxes and is able to operate more

Figure 1.3 Losing coherence: sensory chaos

effectively. We shall do this by reducing the sensory clutter that the brain finds so difficult and painful to process, while at the same time introducing landmarks (such as elements of its own body language), ones that are so familiar and hard-wired in that it recognises them without having to put them through the processing system.

This may sound complicated – but once we understand what we are doing and why, it is remarkably simple. The outcome is a reduction in distressed behaviour and an increase in the ability to attend and relate, even in those children and adults at the extreme end of the autistic spectrum. However, first of all we need to look at what it means to be autistic. After we have looked at this we shall turn our attention to the mechanics of Intensive Interaction and Sensory Integration – what do we actually do to help people?

Meeting a large number of people on the autistic spectrum it is quite clear that, although there are some who we might describe as typically autistic, there is also an enormous range of ways that autism shows itself, especially when what are known as 'autistic tendencies' are allied to severe learning disability or some of the genetic syndromes.

While there are many books on autism, one of the problems is that most of these are written to look at how we can cope with the care problems it presents. Even those books written by people with autism are by people who have speech. They speak for people who are articulate and able to manage their autism, but often assume that others who are more vulnerable are the same as themselves. (Putting oneself in the place of others is one of the autistic problems.) The people we have in mind in this handbook are those who are voiceless, distressed, often incontinent and prone to outbursts of extreme behaviour. (I avoid the term 'challenging' deliberately, since, whatever its intent, it is too often taken as confrontational.) We shall make the distinction suggested by Donna Williams (who is autistic) which distinguishes between an *outside-in approach*, the viewpoint of the non-autistic partner looking at the consequences of autism for care, and an *inside-out approach*, which takes the viewpoint of the partner with autism and their sensory experience of being on the spectrum.[3]

Most of all we must remember that each person with autism is first and foremost an individual. What we are calling 'autism' is laid on top of their personality. So how does it feel to be autistic and what are the particular problems that arise from the experience of autism?

---

3   Williams (1996).

2

A Different Sensory Experience

DO YOU SEE WHAT I SEE?

While it used to be thought that we should not listen to what people with autism were saying about their condition (because it was said that their brains were not working normally so any account they gave was bound to be skewed), we now have many articulate, illuminating and often remarkably consistent reports in the form of books, audiotapes and film which give us a good picture of the range of experience that is known as autism.

Just as important, if we enter the doorway that people with autism have opened, it leads us into a place where we can engage with our autistic partners. We can not only be in their world, but also offer them safe passage into ours. Effectively (and affectively) this enables us to build a bridge between our two worlds so that we can engage with each other in partnership. We can learn from them and they can learn from us.

We all of us live in a sensory world. Whether we are autistic or *neurotypical* (not autistic), we are dependent on the impressions picked up by our eyes, nose, mouth, ears and skin. In addition, our brains also receive messages through our *proprioceptive* and *vestibular systems*. (Muscular and balance sensations that tell us where we are and what we are doing in space. If you stand on your toes you will feel the tension in the muscles in the back of your legs. This is a proprioceptive signal from sensors in the calf muscles.) As well as this we have internal sensations of hunger and fullness and emotional feedback that informs us how we feel. All these inputs get channelled back into the brain. The brain sieves out what is important from what is unimportant and processes our sensory impressions to build up a wider picture of what is happening. It then sets in motion how we should react.

To sum up, if it is working properly, our sensory processing system is the brain's operational director. It detects, registers and analyses the thrust and detail of an input and organises and adjusts our reaction, resulting in a behavioural response. In people with ASD (autistic spectrum disorder), the senses themselves may be working perfectly well but there are problems both in the sifting and in the processing system. Such distortions mean that our autistic partner may get an altered perception of the reality we share: in terms of the world round them, they may see, hear, feel, smell, taste and get a completely different picture to those not on the spectrum. For example:

- a room may suddenly change its apparent size
- a shower can feel like red-hot needles jabbing into the skin
- our partner may not know where they are in space or even if they are the right way up, becoming anxious when their feet are off the ground, for example when stepping off the kerb
- the straight line between the wall and floor may wriggle.

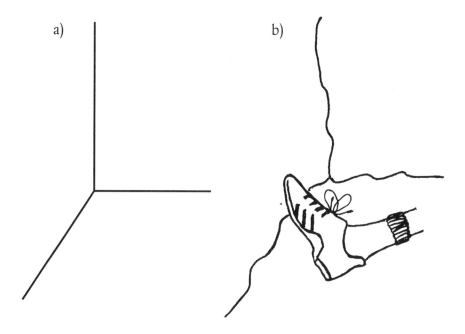

Figure 2.1 John is not naughty. He kicks the wall to know where it is. He is checking up on distorted visual perception by using touch.
a) Neurotypical perception of walls and floor
b) Autistic perception of walls and floor

OVERWHELMING SENSORY EXPERIENCE

People on the spectrum say that they feel as if they are living in a world that constantly threatens to overwhelm them. Many will say that they live in fear, not just of what is happening but that something terrible may happen. Also, if the brain has made a faulty assessment of the situation, the individual may feel they are being threatened even when they are not.

It is one thing to read about and acknowledge this sensory discrepancy between our sensory perception and that of our partners with autism but it is quite another to take it on board, to actually feel how they feel. We need a picture to help us.

Think of a busy airport. If too many planes come in they stack up and circle round, waiting for space to land. So in the autistic brain, if too many sensory impressions are coming in, they circle round in the brain unattached and unprocessed, overlapping and interfering with each other.

Back to the airport: suppose now that there is a bomb scare in another terminal. Diverted planes add to the confusion at ours. The air traffic controller decides he cannot manage, switches off his radar screen and goes home. The outcome is chaos: confusion, crashes, pain and heat.

So also, if the autistic brain is subjected to more sensory information than it can process, it is overtaken by an *autonomic storm*,[1] also known as *fragmentation* or *meltdown*. All the sensory impressions break up, parts of the brain shut down and the body experiences 'confusion', 'pain', 'agony' and 'terror', although not everybody goes through this in the same measure. Children will say:

'My head is switched off.'

'My head is running away.'

'I am wearing my silly head today.'

'I have got my wrong head on.'

'I am exploding from inside.'

'Death is coming to get me.'

'Pain, pain, pain!'

'I will do anything to stop it. I'll run in front of a car, bash my head on the wall.'

---

1   The autonomic nervous system controls our body systems such as breathing, sweating and heartbeat rate but is not normally under conscious control. An 'autonomic storm' is a term introduced by Ramachandran (2006) to describe the state where the autonomic nervous system runs wild. It has extremely unpleasant physical effects.

We need to listen extremely carefully to what people on the autistic spectrum are writing about their condition, so that we do not judge the behaviour of the less articulate (or build our strategies) on the basis of our own version of reality. If we don't hear what they are saying, we shall get it wrong.

Key points

- People on the autistic spectrum experience the sensory world differently from those who are not on the spectrum.
- The autistic brain does not process sensory input in the same way as the non-autistic brain. In the event of too much sensory input all at once, the autistic brain may experience overload. At the extremes of overload, images, sounds and feelings break up into fragments and the person experiences what is now called an autonomic storm.
- We can, and must, learn about their experience of the world from what they say about it, rather than by making behavioural judgements and basing our strategies on our own *sensory experience*.

3

Alternative Viewpoints

LOOKING FROM THE OUTSIDE IN

We know from people who are writing about their autism that they experience the world we all share in a different way – and also that we, who are looking from the outside, see autism quite differently to the way they do. This leads us to take approaches that are based on our own experience of sensory reality. As we mentioned in Chapter 1, Donna Williams makes the distinction between an 'outside-in' approach and an 'inside-out' approach.

From our point of view, autism is often summed up as a *triad of impairments*:

1. failure to relate

2. failure to think flexibly

3. failure to understand speech.

People on the spectrum are seen in terms of this three-point failure, although a recent survey of the total population, autistic and non-autistic, suggests that these traits are widespread and in different combinations and perhaps are better thought of as – and treated as – individual traits, rather than lumping them all together.[1]

Typically from the outsider's point of view, what we notice about people with severe autism is:

1. an impaired ability to engage, either through speech or through non-verbal engagement; withdrawal

2. attention focused on a particular activity, clinging to routine

3. outbursts of unmanageable behaviour, sometimes called *tantrums*.

These outbursts may be accompanied by bellowing, screaming, biting, scratching, spitting, hitting themselves on walls and sometimes attacking anything nearby, furniture or people. It is at this stage that we tend to feel helpless and sometimes despairing. How can we possibly cope with or manage (or help them to manage) the lives of partners who appear to be tearing themselves and their world apart?[2]

LOOKING FROM THE INSIDE OUT

So far we have looked at autism from the point of view of cognitive failure, a point of view that leads us to search for the bits of the brain that are not working. Now we are going to turn our attention to a sensory viewpoint (how autism *feels*) and look at the same picture from the standpoint of the person with autism. For example, take the intake of visual stimuli – what we see.

---

1   Happé, Ronald and Plomin (2006).

2   Donna Williams has introduced the idea of looking at autism from the inside in her book *Autism: An Inside-Out Approach* (1996).

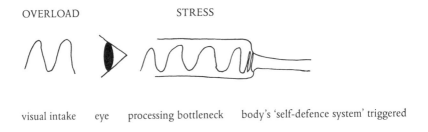

OVERLOAD   STRESS

visual intake   eye   processing bottleneck   body's 'self-defence system' triggered

COPING STRATEGIES
- repetitive behaviour
- exit strategies
  ◦ avoidance
  ◦ aggression
  ◦ freezing

AUTONOMIC STORM = FRAGMENTATION
Disturbances in the autonomic nervous system. Images break up into fragments. Note that this experience involves the sensations of real pain, confusion and sometimes heat.

Figure 3.1 Onset of overload and autonomic storm

From the point of view of the person with autism there appear to be three phases in the development of a full-blown sensory processing breakdown. The first is known as *sensory overload*, too much of which leads to *break-up* or *fragmentation* of sensory impressions in an autonomic storm. In order to avoid reaching this stage our partner develops *coping strategies* as an attempt to restore sensory equilibrium and hold on to some idea of what is happening.

OVERLOAD

If we consider sensory breakup in terms of vision, the visual images that we see enter our eyes in the form of waves. On the way to the brain these waves hit a processing bottleneck that, whatever its exact mechanism, this results in *build-up* or *overload* (the term depends on whose account you are reading). If the sensory overload becomes too great, the person will tip over into fragmentation or the autonomic storm with all its horrible sensations.

Timing may be important. Any delay in processing, response and decoding of incoming information can result in an input that is 'out of sync' with its context (and therefore meaningless), giving rise to confusion and anxiety and raising the level of stress. On top of this, inconsistencies in the ability to register an input mean that some days a person may tolerate an experience but is unable to do so on others. If the processing system is already full of input, the slightest trigger may cause overload.

THE AUTONOMIC STORM

We know something of the experience of what it feels like to be subject to an autonomic storm from the writings of a number of authors who are on the spectrum.

> When they saw the sound of a moped made me act strangely they started scaring me. They would wait for me to pass them and then suddenly rev up. The din made the ground under my feet disappear and I could neither see nor feel the world around me. Up and down were suddenly in the same place and I had no idea where my feet were. So as not to fall over or explode from inside, I had to grab the fence where I was standing, pressing myself against it and holding on hard. I had to feel something that stood still, something anchored in a world that had become totally unpredictable. (Gunilla Gerland)[3]

> All the time I was growing up I experienced a constant shudder down my spine. Periodically the shuddering grew worse while at other times it kept relatively quiet so I could live with it. It was like that feeling before you sneeze, only as if it had got stuck and was suspended inside my spine in order to turn into something permanent... I became slightly used to it but it was a constant torture, most noticeable when it changed in intensity. It was like

3   Gerland (1996).

cold steel down my spine. It was hard and fluid at the same time, with metallic fingers drumming and tickling the outside. Like sharp clips digging into my spine and lemonade inside. Icy heat and digging fiery cold. It was like the sound of screeching chalk against a blackboard turned into a silent concentration of feeling, then placed in the back of my neck. From there, so metallic, the feeling radiated out into my arms, clipped itself firmly into my elbows, but never came to an end. Never ever came to an end. (Gunilla Gerland)[4]

A feeling kept washing over me. It began with the feeling one gets from eating lemons. It was like a tingling in the back of the neck. It spread to every fibre of my body like cracks in an earthquake. I knew this monster. It was the Big Black nothingness and it felt like death coming to get me. The walls went up and my ears hurt. I had to get out, out of the room, out of this thing stuck on me, suffocating me inside my shell of flesh. A scream rose in my throat. My four year old legs ran from one side of the room, moving ever faster and faster, my body hitting the wall like a sparrow flying at the window. My body was shaking. Here it was. Death was here. Don't want to die, don't want to die, don't want to die…the repetition of the words blended into a pattern with only one word standing out, the word die. My knees went to the floor. My hands ran down the mirror. My eyes frantically searched the eyes looking back, looking for meaning, looking for something to connect. No-one, nothing, nowhere. Silent screaming rose in my throat. My head seemed to explode. My chest heaved with each final breath at the gates of death. Dizziness and exhaustion began to overtake the terror. It was amazing how many times a day I could be dying and still be alive. (Donna Williams)[5]

Both Gunilla and Donna describe a feeling in the spine which starts as a fizzy sensation (like lemons or lemonade) in the back of the neck and

---

4 Gerland (1996).

5 Williams (1992).

spreads outwards to the extremities of the body. We often see people rubbing or hitting themselves on the head and back of the neck in an attempt to desensitise themselves when they are starting to become upset. (Occasionally a cold wet towel on the nape of the neck can help desensitise this sensation at this stage. The towel must be really cold and offered immediately.)

Exactly where people are on the overload/fragmentation scale seems to vary from one description to another. If we look at Gunilla Gerland's accounts of her childhood experience, she seems to be talking about ongoing low-level sensations that vary in intensity as well as overwhelming surges of sensation. One can imagine this as like being the difference between a glitch on the television and the screen blowing out.

In a desperate effort to have some sort of idea of what is going on round them, to *maintain coherence* and to avoid going into fragmentation, the autistic brain develops *coping strategies*.

COPING STRATEGIES

Because of its terrifying physical effects, the one thing that our partners want to avoid is tipping from overload into an autonomic storm. Broadly speaking, coping strategies fall into one of two types: repetitive behaviours and exit strategies.

1. Repetitive behaviours and themes

Some people with severe autism focus on a repetitive behaviour all the time. This may be difficult to spot – as little as their own breathing rhythm, or a particular click made with the tongue. A common repetitive behaviour is scratching the fingers or hands in one way or another.

All these repetitive activities are self-stimulating in what amounts to a conversation between the person's brain and their body. The brain sends a message to the body saying 'Do this', whatever it is, and the body sends *feedback* to the brain in the form of a sensation, saying that it has 'Done it'. However, in the light of the need to maintain coher-

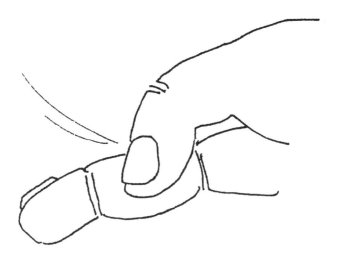

Figure 3.2 Scratching fingers helps to maintain coherence

ence and make sense of chaotic sensory experience, it may be more accurate to think of such behaviours as *self-preservatory* rather than self-stimulatory as such. It's not so much that I am devoted to the sensation of my thumb scratching my finger as that, under circumstances which the brain perceives as life-threatening (losing touch with my ability to process – 'my head is running away'), when I do this I am giving myself a sensation that my brain recognises.

Because the brain has difficulty in planning new movements – and also has problems in switching off – this brain–body cycle may be repeated over and over again until it is 'hard-wired in' (perseveration). One might think of this in terms of the worn-down bed of a stream, where it becomes easier and easier for the water to take the same path.

The person with autism can focus on this internal conversation to the exclusion of external and intrusive inputs, what Donna Williams calls the 'Blah-blah' out there. All their focus is directed to trying to make sense of their world by cutting down on the volume of sensory input to which they have to attend, filtering out the excess, maintaining coherence, at the same time fine-tuning on the repetitive sensory behaviour to the point at which it becomes ingrained. Rather than focusing on an internally derived sensation, other people will get their stimulus from an activity that they hijack from the world outside themselves, using it to feed their inner world. Common examples of this *fixated* behaviour vary from simply re-arranging the furniture, opening and shutting a cupboard door or tearing paper to the more sophisticated *themes* of watching certain videos, lining up cars and taking part in activities such as obsessions with trains, science fiction or computers.

People with autism say that when they focus on a repetitive behaviour, it is a point of reference which helps them to cut out overloading signals. It is a predictable activity: they know what they are doing and it helps them to feel secure.

Another way to cut down on overload is for the brain to 'shut down' one of the senses. Donna Williams describes how she went through periods when she could either 'see' or 'feel' but not do both at the same time. For example, she could either see her hand but not feel it was attached to her, or feel it but not see it was part of her. So her hand was a thing floating in front of her, apparently detached. While some people may be getting too little information from their muscles, in others, during the break-up that accompanies an autonomic storm, the *proprioceptive* (internal muscular) sensations remain intact, while the other senses melt away in the confusion.

When we come to use Intensive Interaction we shall want to tap into the brain–body internal feedback, the internal messaging which is part of the brain's familiar repertoire and instantly recognisable, since for our partner it is user-friendly and does not threaten to overload the brain. We are going to use this to move our partner's attention from solitary self-stimulation to an activity we can share.

It will also be important to look at how a person is doing their activity, since it is the *how* that tells us what they are feeling, for example whether they are calm or upset.

2. Exit strategies

An alternative way to using repetitive behaviours to avoid going into fragmentation is to get out of the situation which is, rightly or wrongly, seen to be the cause of sensory overload. One can either do this by physically cutting out the source by hiding, putting the hands over the ears, shutting the eyes, turning away, running out of the room, pulling clothes or a blanket over the head to cut down on sensory input, or drown the particular frequency which is hurting by listening to a louder but different sound. The alternative is to lash out at the person whom one perceives as the cause of the sensory overload. Get rid of them.

So in order to reduce overloading sensory input we have *avoidance* and *aggression*, two of the classic responses to triggering the body's self-defence system. (The third response, *freezing*, does very occasionally arise in the form of catatonia, when our partner simply comes to a halt and will remain fixed in that position like a frightened rabbit. Alternatively they may be completely trapped in a particular behaviour such as crying or laughing which has nothing to do with how they are feeling.)

What we need to understand is that in people with autism, the threshold for triggering the self-defence system is extremely low, almost floor level.

Our partner may start by trying to maintain coherence by focusing on a repetitive behaviour. As the stress increases this will become increasingly agitated. If this does not help they may move on to exit strategies and, lastly, trying to run away or aggression. Some people will go straight into attack mode.

Being witness to a person who is going through an autonomic storm is frightening because of our helplessness and the potential danger to the individual concerned as well as ourselves. *It is vital to understand that the reason this happens is because they are experiencing sensory overload.* They simply cannot deal with what is going on in their brain which is constantly telling them that they are in mortal danger. They feel as if they are being attacked and therefore respond as if this is the case.

Sometimes people with autism can tolerate more stimulation than at others. Whether or not they pass from overload to an autonomic storm appears to depend on how stressed the brain is at any particular time. The more stressed the brain is, the more likely the person with autism is likely to tip over the edge. The less stressed it is, the easier it is for people to process their sensory intake (see Figure 3.1).

Key points

- Too much sensory input of the wrong sort leads to a bottleneck in the processing system.
- If there is too much pressure on the bottleneck, the sensory impressions break up into fragments and the person experiences the 'autonomic storm'.
- To avoid its unpleasant and painful effects (interpreted sometimes as life-threatening) the individual develops coping strategies.
- Coping strategies include focusing on repetitive behaviours or trying to get out of the situation, either by hiding from the trigger or trying to eliminate what is seen to be, whether or not it is, the source of distress.
- It is this latter situation that leads to so much of what is known as *challenging behaviour* but which I prefer to call *distressed behaviour* since it is clearly the outcome of stress.
- We have to be careful with the language we use since it colours the way we think.

4

Sensory Distress and its Causes

A PAINFUL EXPERIENCE

There are many triggers for sensory distress and the stress this causes in the lives of people with autistic spectrum disorder. Feedback to the triggers is variously described on a range from 'confusion' and 'discomfort' to 'agony'. What we have to realise is that if we knowingly subject our partners to a sensory trigger to which they are sensitive we may be seriously hurting them. The hunt for these triggers should be top of our priority list. Once we understand that behaviours that seem to us bizarre are usually attempts by our partner to self-regulate by bringing coherence into a world that seems chaotic to them, it is not so difficult.

In order to find the triggers to these behaviours (which will be different for each of our partners) we need to study them with great care. Why does Jim swing on the curtains in a particular way? How does the physical feedback he is giving himself have meaning for him? Is it that he is trying to correct a difficulty he is having with his balance system? And why does Matty, who is a bright child with extreme sensory distress, refuse to use PECS (Picture Exchange Communication System; it involves the exchange of images on flash cards for objects or activities) but is happy to use a pointing board? What is it about PECS that is so threatening that he cannot bear to use it? It is not that he does not want to communicate, so what is the difference? Can it be the sound of tearing velcro? We have to learn to think round corners and ask ourselves each time: what's in it for our partner?

People with autism describe the sensations they experience in a variety of ways:

> 'It's like being tuned into twenty television sets at once, with a faulty volume control. Sorting out what is happening at any time is a fulltime occupation.' (Lindsey Weekes)[1]

> 'It's like having a lion in the head.' (Temple Grandin)[2]

> 'I spend my whole life trying to work out what is going on.' (Thérèse Jolliffe)[3]

> 'I have no idea what is going to happen in five minutes' time or what happened five minutes ago.' (Donna Williams)[4]

It is not just that the past is forgotten and the future unpredictable; even the present is murky and tinged with fear, fear of being in a situation which causes pain. Because the brain is having difficulty processing incoming information, life walks on a knife edge, in constant fear of the unknown and also of being tipped into the autonomic storm.

---

1   Weekes (date unknown) in *A Bridge of Voices*.

2   Grandin in Arnall and Peters (1992).

3   Joliffe, Lansdown and Robinson (1992).

4   Williams (1995).

TWO LEVELS OF DISTRESS

The effect of sensory distress is that our partners very often have no idea where they are and what they are doing.

If we pay attention to what they are telling us, there appear to be two levels of distress. The first is a low-level background clutter or static, which is normally present and, as Gunilla Gerland says, 'I slightly got used to it – even if it was torture'.[5] But then there are also the crisis points, the 'storms', when everything in the mind blows.

What can be misleading from the outsider's point of view is that sometimes a person can manage a situation without becoming upset but, at other times, the same situation will trigger an outburst. (We are apt to make behavioural judgements about this. We see our partners as being 'difficult' or a child as 'lazy' or 'naughty', since we know that the person can do whatever it is sometimes.) As we gain experience in working with our partner, it becomes clear that the crucial factor in determining whether or not they are able to respond or whether they will go into fragmentation is the level of stress they are experiencing. If they are experiencing low levels of stress they are less likely to fragment. If their stress levels are high, they easily tip into fragmentation. So we need to look at what it is that triggers stress in people with autism.

FACTORS CAUSING STRESS

Broadly speaking, and although they overlap, we can divide the stress triggers into:

- sensory distortions
- emotional overload
- confusing messages
- hormonal problems.

---

5   Gerland (1996).

Sensory distortions come from what might be described as a bottleneck in the information processing system. Incoming signals from the world outside are not in sync with the rate at which they can be processed. This can be due to hypersensitivity to external signals in any of the senses – vision, sound, touch, taste, smell and balance. With hyposensitivity the problem is when the brain is not receiving enough of a signal. There also seems to be a more generalised confusion overloading the system. Exactly how this works is not clear yet, but our partners are getting a very scrambled view of the world we share.

Emotional overload is best thought of as a hypersensitivity to internal sensations and feedback. What we, as non-autistic partners, might feel as a pleasant sensation of warmth when a friend smiles at us is experienced as a tidal wave of overwhelming and often unpleasant sensations instead. There are a number of factors involved here. First of all it is wrong to think that people with autism do not 'feel'. Far from not feeling, people with ASD may be hypersensitive to internal emotions. As mentioned in the Introduction, Thérèse Jolliffe says, 'We do love people, we do feel lonely', but adds that what is difficult to cope with is the feedback that she gets back from her own body. She feels that she is drowning.

By *confusing messages*, we mean what Donna Williams calls the 'Blah-blah' that comes from 'out there'. Sounds without meaning, no more significant than noise. For example, the level of interpretation required to decode people's speech is phenomenal for the person with autism – there are so many messages to take account of. Speech is essentially a minefield.

Finally, stress can be caused and/or exacerbated by *hormonal factors*. Donna Williams tells us that the hormonal surges experienced during puberty are overwhelming, particularly for boys. Again, they feel as if they are being attacked and respond as if this is so. Clinical observation suggests that, during puberty, children become more sensitive to those effects that were already triggering distress. We need to pay even more attention to providing quiet surroundings, using functional communication systems that have meaning for our partners and exploring the use of body language to put ourselves in tune with them.

We must emphasise that each person with autism is different and not everyone on the spectrum will be sensitive to all the triggers listed. We are looking at a very 'pick-and-mix' situation. Also our partners will experience the different sensitivities in varying degrees depending on the severity of the autism. However, the picture is not entirely hopeless. We can help people, even those with very severe autism, as we shall see in later chapters – but first we need to know what the problems are likely to be. It is our task to sort out in which sensory areas our particular partner is sensitive.

The first three of the four categories of factors causing stress require further elaboration. Therefore, we will now look at sensory distortions, emotional overload and confusing messages in a more in-depth way in the following chapters.

Key points

- Children and adults on the autistic spectrum experience an overwhelming assault of sensory distress, both from external and internal sources.
- They may experience hypersensitivity (acute over-stimulation from sensory input) or hyposensitivity (under-stimulation from sensory input).

5

Sensory Distortions

Chapter contents

HYPERSENSITIVITIES

What do we mean by hypersensitivity? We tend to think of hypersensitivity as a sensation that we neurotypicals experience – but a bit more so. This is not the case. If I was hypersensitive to sound and stood beside you, I would be able to hear the blood pumping in *your* veins. A man asked to compare the pain of his light hypersensitivity with that of his kidney stones (notoriously painful) rated the kidney stones at five out of ten but sensitivity to light at eight out of ten. We need to understand that the autistic experience of hypersensitivity is right off the end of our scale. We do not know how violent the assault of these feelings can be.

Hypersensitivities can occur in any of the senses. Contrary to current perception, the latest count of senses numbers them at 21. This figure includes both senses that receive inputs from the outside world – such as vision, sound, touch, smell, taste and balance – and internal sensations such as desire and embarrassment and other visceral feelings. Also included are proprioceptive signals which come from the sensors on our muscles and internal organs. Hyposensitivity is when the person is not getting enough of the signal to make sense of its message. This happens most often in relation to the internal muscular feelings or proprioception. Apart from hyper- and hypo-sensitivities, we may also be looking at more generalised sensory distortions, for example, such as lack of consistency and size shifting. For example, the dimensions of a room may suddenly shrink. Basically the brain is presenting a distorted view of the world we share.

VISION

Of all the sensory disturbances, most is known about those affecting vision. A small boy says his eyes play tricks on him. Sometimes they work and sometimes they do not. This visual distortion is known as *Irlen syndrome* or *scotopic sensitivity*. Everything goes squiggly and moves around. People describe it as like a glitch on the TV, like looking into a distorting mirror, or living in a kaleidoscope where the bits swirl round and the pattern never settles. Alongside this (and perhaps in an effort to deal with it) is the problem that the eye tends to pick up details and miss the whole picture. Sometimes a child will try and frame what he sees by looking through a small aperture.

> Donna Williams says she sees the parts but not the whole, the leaves but not the tree.[1]

---

1   Williams (1992).

Ros Blackburn, who is also autistic, says she sees objects without context. It is like seeing everything through a tube. She sees the light switch but not the light switch to turn on the kitchen light.[2]

Irlen syndrome is not confined to people on the autistic spectrum. It can be triggered (in some people on the spectrum) by intensity of light, by certain patterns and by particular colours. (The particular colours are specific for an individual.)

Intensity of light

Quite a large proportion of people with ASD will screw their eyes up, particularly in bright light. Or they will keep their hands over their eyes or choose to sit in darkened rooms. If they are doing this it is because they find bright light painful.

> Since his behaviour is so aggressive, a man has to have four people supervising him all the time. He sits on a sofa opposite a window with his eyes screwed up. Occasionally he looks at the floor over the end of the sofa. His eyes are wide open and relaxed. Moving the sofa so that he is no longer looking straight into the light results in a marked drop in aggressive outbursts.

Do not use fluorescent lighting. Avoid seating people in bright light and looking out of windows. In particular, make sure that children are not seated at brightly coloured or white workstations if they are involved in the TEACCH method. Fluorescent light can be particularly painful, especially when bouncing off a bright surface. Try using dimmer switches so they can alter the light themselves. (This may seem a small adjustment but with some people it can make a great difference to behaviour.)

---

2   Blackburn (2004).

Pattern

We try to make our houses cheerful. Many have high levels of sensory stimulus, patterned wallpaper, patterned carpets, patterned upholstery, all demanding processing. Pictures on the walls and ornaments all contribute to the visual chaos which can overwhelm someone with autism.

> A man refuses to go home when his mother changes the carpet from plain to patterned. She buys a different, plain one and he returns.

> A woman bangs her head on the black carpet blotches, and spits on the dark knots in the wood of the table and the edges of furniture where the light reflects. She then rubs the saliva in an effort to erase the source which is disturbing her.

> A man thumps his support worker only on days when the support worker wears a black jersey with white zig-zag. This behaviour stops when the support worker no longer wears this jumper to work.

> A woman repeatedly removes the pictures from her wall.

All these people are protesting against visual overload. Think tranquillity when decorating.

Colour

Much more research needs to be done in this field but evidence is mounting that some people on the autistic spectrum can process visual information much more easily in certain colours.

> In Birmingham University Education Department, changes in the behaviour of autistic children are filmed in a grey room with variable lighting. Marked differences are noted in response to different coloured lights. (Although it is not always a red/green contrast, in the videos I have seen, in red light the children turned away from a teacher and in green light they welcomed them.)

In a resource play area two out of six autistic children behave better in green light than in red. In red light they wandered round staring at the lights. In green light they came and sat down and were co-operative.

An autistic child calms down when he is placed in a blue room.

It is easy to confuse 'fixating' with 'liking'. Support people often think that their partner 'likes something' such as eye contact when actually they are fixating on this, using it to maintain coherence. If one interrupts a fixation one is likely to be attacked. Our partners are more likely to enjoy sharing something they like.

A man trashes his room daily. This behaviour stops completely when the walls and all his furnishings are changed to pale dull green.

A child is behaving badly in the sandpit area. At lunch I heard the supervisor in the kitchen say, 'Don't give him a yellow or red plate, he'll throw his lunch on the floor.' It turns out that the play area is lined with brilliant fluorescent orange tiles.

A mum gives her son a fluorescent green rug to cheer up his room. Every day he throws it out and she tells him to put it back. Once she realises the problem he has with its colour she throws it away.

But on the other hand:

Before lunch a small boy runs out of his class and picks a red chair to put in his place. He is very upset if teachers insist he has a grey one. For this child, when he has the red chair to sit on, he knows what he's doing.

Investigations into Irlen syndrome (scotopic sensitivity) on people on the autistic spectrum arose out of investigations into dyslexia when it became clear that a proportion of people with dyslexia were helped by wearing coloured lenses. Some people with autism realised that, for them, it was not just letters or numbers jumping around but everything.

Donna Williams said that when she first put her Irlen lenses on, 'everything sort of went shunt' and she thought, 'Oh my God, that's what everybody else is seeing.' It cut down the number of 'floating' unattached images in her brain and made it easier to work out what was happening. When she took them off the confusion returned, 'everything sort of slides away'.[3] A man who is non-verbal responds to coloured lenses by lifting his head. His jaw drops and he looks round the room as if seeing the world for the first time.

A comparison of drawings, made when our partner is wearing and not wearing coloured lenses, shows massive differences in what they can see of their surroundings. First, a child is asked to draw what he sees in a room when he is not wearing his glasses. He draws a bunch of flowers. When he puts on his glasses, this bunch of flowers turns out to be a stencil on the back of the toilet. Now he can see, he draws the whole toilet, a bath with taps, the door with handle and the medicine cabinet with the bottles with their tops.

When not wearing his coloured lenses, all the boy sees is the bunch of flowers. He fixates on these in order to see something. He knows that if he needs to go to the toilet he must put his knee near the bunch of flowers.[4] The implications of this, particularly for teaching, are enormous. A person with Irlen syndrome may focus on one object in a room and see nothing else at all.

To summarise what is known about Irlen syndrome:

- Although it arises in the normal population it is more common among people on the autistic spectrum.

- Some people with autism who have visual distortions are helped by using coloured lenses.

- Such visual processing problems do not show up in an ordinary eye test. Testing must be done by a qualified practitioner.

- Although the people I have worked with are usually better in green light or sometimes blue light, this is not always the case.

---

3   Donna Williams in *Jam-Jar* (1995), *Autism: An Inside-Out Approach* (1996) and *Like Colour to the Blind* (1998).

4   Verbal communication, Ann Wright, Irlen Centre.

The optimum colour is different for different people. The wrong colour lens can make distortions worse.

- More research needs to be done.

- Some people on the autistic spectrum, particularly those who are unable to cope with optical testing, can sometimes be helped by using coloured light bulbs. Try green or blue and monitor for behavioural change. (Note that if a person functions best in pink lenses, they will need a green light bulb and vice versa. We are looking at the opposite end of the colour spectrum.)

- The appropriate-coloured light can be clipped to a work desk to throw a pool of light onto the work area.

- Screwed-up eyes are an indication of scotopic sensitivity, especially in bright light, as also is preference for dim light and for a particular colour or dislike of a particular colour.

It seems possible that the capacity to process is not individual for each sense. If we cut down the sensory input in one mode, say vision, it can sometimes help a person to process a different mode. For example, Donna Williams says that when she is wearing her coloured lenses she can also hear better.

SOUND

Sounds are unreliable: sometimes they are loud and sometimes they fade away completely.

'Even my own voice booms at me.'

'Sometimes when the toilet is flushed it is like a train going to run over me.'[5]

A child tells his mother that sometimes the sound of a snowflake falling is like breaking glass.

---

5   Both quotes taken from *A is for Autism* (Grandin in Arnall and Peters 1992).

Sounds do not have to be loud in order to cause disturbance and pain. They are also very individual: for example, a ballpoint click-pen, metal cutlery on a plate, the sound of heating or air conditioning.

Certain sounds (usually high frequencies) hurt. *Hyperacusis* is an acute and painful sensitivity to sound. The same sound may sometimes cause pain and sometimes not. Hypersensitivity to sound is often worse in one ear. Sometimes a cotton wool plug in one ear may help since the other ear can hear perfectly.

> On video one can spot that a child flinches when his partner makes one of his sounds from his right side.

It appears this hypersensitivity is a purely physical problem:

> A man is extremely aggressive when he hears certain sounds. His audiologist makes him a hearing aid mould, drills a hole in it and fills the hole with an acoustic material which cuts out the frequencies which he is sensitive to. His behavioural difficulties cease.[6]

If we realise our partner finds a particular sound impossible (for example if they become disturbed when the telephone rings), it is sensible not to subject them to this sound, because we are causing them pain; we need to chage the ringtone. Desensitisation is particularly difficult and not often successful. Even if our partner does apparently 'get used' to the sound, it may still cause them stress, not just when it happens but also in anticipation that it *may* happen. This adds to their low-level stress and makes it more likely that they will tip into fragmentation, the autonomic storm.

One of the characteristics of autism is that the brain does not switch off easily and so sound messages get stuck in a persistent loop that goes on and on; called 'perseveration', this sound (or other unprocessed stimulus) may go on in the head all day.

> A man who has breakfast in a noisy room goes into his room afterwards and beats his head on the wall for up to ten hours, the

---

6   Verbal communication from Michael Brown, consultant audiologist, Lancaster Royal Infirmary.

time that the noisy sounds continue to echo in his head. This behaviour ends when he is given breakfast in a quiet area.

Sometimes there are conflicting messages running in opposite directions and the person becomes extremely upset.

A man knows that a bus comes to the door before dinner but he does not understand intervals. In the time between the arrival of the bus and dinner being put on the table he starts to bellow and bite himself. (The logic of this is 'dinner comes after the bus, dinner is not here'.) Fortunately he enjoys walks so he is taken out before the bus arrives and not brought back until dinner is on the table. This is the end of this particular problem.

Always speak quietly.[7] Your partner is far more likely to be able to process what you are saying and you are far more likely to be understood if you never raise your voice.

TOUCH AND BOUNDARIES

What most of us normally think of as 'touch' is not just one sense but two: we sense the world through our skin (heat/cold and pressure) but also receive the muscular sensations that derive from movement and internal pressure. If I press my thumb on the table, I not only feel the smooth surface of the table (*tactile response*) but also get an internal sensation of pressure on the joints in my thumb (*proprioceptive response*).

Proprioception is about processing our internal muscular and joint feelings and is a term that refers to information received when muscles stretch or contract and joints bend, straighten, pull or compress. Most proprioceptive input is processed unconsciously. Perhaps surprisingly it has a critical role in modulating our emotional states and influencing our motor actions, so that we may occasionally bang doors or stamp our feet if we are angry. The proprioceptive system works together with touch and movement but it requires active resistance from our muscles and joints. Some people will bite, push, bump, bang and hurl

---

7   Gail Gillingham: 'Look for visual and auditory tranquillity' (Gillingham 1995).

objects in their attempts to increase proprioceptive input. Some will even attack their care staff in order to obtain restraint and consequent pressure. Conversely, according to Blairs and Slater, deep pressure such as a firm bear hug can be effective in reducing anxiety-related 'challenging behaviour' with a consequent reduction in medication and physical restraint.[8]

Whereas firm pressure from the hands can be reassuring, a light brush can be very painful and distressing.

'It feels like a whole load of spiders trying to crawl out of my skin.' (Unnamed child)

Tactile defensiveness is the tendency to react negatively to touch sensations. Most of us will pull away from a touch that takes us by surprise but a child who is tactile defensive is over-reactive to stimuli which most of us would not respond to. It is difficult to pay attention to your environment if you are overly sensitive to the feelings of the materials of the clothes on your skin or the hair on your head.

Pressure sensations seem to balance out excessive sensitivity in the tactile system. We rub hard on the place where we have bumped ourselves. The sensation of deep pressure helps to block the flow of pain impulses.

Sensory Integration Therapy uses firm pressure to help children develop a sense of their bodies and boundaries, something that is absent in many people with autism, who, for example, may not realise their hand is attached to them and have no idea of where they stop and other people begin. Famously Temple Grandin devised a squeeze machine based on a cattle press (machinery to hold cattle still during branding) designed to desensitise the painful stimuli she felt in her skin.

Both firm and light pressure are received as stimuli through the skin, so can the brain manage to process deep pressure felt in the muscles but not light touch felt through tactile sensors in the skin? Jane Horwood suggests that it is better to think about how the brain processes the localisation of where that touch has occurred.

---

8   Blairs and Slater (2007).

If touch is firm and maintained for approximately six seconds then the combination of the tactile and proprioceptive receptors aids processing, partly by the modulating influence of the proprioceptive system. Light touch is much more difficult to localise and initially is alerting and stimulating. Once it has occurred, the brain may be too bombarded with other stimuli unable to filter what had just happened.

Tactile impulses appear to be received in many areas of the brain and touch assists in the organisation of sensation in the brain. Without a great deal of tactile stimulation the brain tends to be unpredictable and unbalanced in its responses to sensory input. Not enough touch can increase tactile defensiveness. Children who are tactile defensive still need a great deal of tactile input and often crave it but it needs to be controlled and combined with deep pressure input.

The tactile system that is involved in the face and head is different from the body's tactile system. Sensory defensiveness around the face and head may be more severe in its responses to tactile input. For example a child may scream when his hair is touched. Sometimes it is helpful to give deep massage of a child's head and scalp before their hair is brushed.

Weights and pressure can help some people to focus on where they are when they are not getting strong enough signals from their bodies (hyposensitivity) and becoming lost in confusion.

> A man wears a clothes peg on his finger. Focusing on the 'pain' helps him to maintain coherence. At least he has one reference point which helps him to know what is happening.

> A child walks on her toes and flaps her arms. She is trying to give herself a feeling strong enough to know where she is in space.

> A child who sits on his own and cannot join in 'circle time' is able to do so if he has previously had a vigorous session on the trampoline.

> A child who cannot cross the road can do so when he is given heavy shopping bags to carry. Another carries a rucksack with a book in to help him know where he is. A third, who likes play dough and lies down on the threshold of his house when he

comes from outside, can walk straight in if given a heavy bowl of play dough to carry.

Figure 5.1 Focusing on weight

Some people can only tolerate touch in certain places, such as the palm of hand, the top of the feet or the soles of the feet. Gunilla Gerland tells us that, for her, touch is more tolerable the further it is from her head. If you do have to touch someone who is touch-defensive, let them know by showing or telling them what you are going to do (and waiting to make sure they have understood) before you do so. This gives the body time to prepare. Always use firm touch.

In this context some children and adults can be helped by vibration since it gives a very powerful stimulus to focus on. It is important when this is used to use it intermittently, and not just to leave the vibration unit on. It is the on/off that is the stimulus not the prolonged buzz. Also, problems can arise when attention is switched from personal interaction to focusing on the instrument, the so-called third object. It is not only our partner who may become locked into the sensation:

both of us may lose the affective bridge. And it is mutual attention that is crucial. It is this that makes the difference to the ability to relate. One way of maintaining contact is the introduction of variations so that our partner's brain is kept on the alert and refers back to us constantly to see what we will do next.

> Working with a child who was very floppy and extremely diffi-cult to motivate, I put him on a trampoline and placed the vibra-tion unit underneath the canvas so that the whole surface carried the vibration and also reflected the sound. We developed a terrific game where he was clambering on and off the trampoline in order to catch up with the vibration unit, which I moved from underneath to on top and back again.

> Another child did not like vibration on her back but placed her hands on the vibration unit and stroked it after she heard the sound it made amplified by placing it on a cupboard door that acted as a sounding board.

As a child grows, his sensory systems help him to develop a *body map*, a body 'schema' that contains information about where his body starts and where it stops, the relationship of the parts and all the movements each part can make. If we have a good body map, we can easily judge whether we can squeeze past a person in a crowded room. We are well coordinated. If we do not have a good body map, then we may have difficulties with boundaries. It is difficult to know where you start and where you stop or even that your hand can function independently.

> Donna Williams describes flapping her hand in front of her for two years, a habit that looks like a typical repetitive behaviour until one reads that, in order to process at least some part of her sensory intake, her brain cut out either seeing or feeling. So she could either see her hand and not feel it, or feel it and not see it. So she never got the idea that it was part of her but rather an irritat-ing thing floating in front of her and she was trying to get rid of it.

For a number of people with ASD who are *hyposensitive* to proprioceptive signals, the world round them is so invasive that they withdraw almost completely. In such cases they may be helped by the use of a transparent screen which they can tap so they can check their faulty proprioceptive intake against touch.

A man lives outside. Even in the winter he will only come indoors for meals, throwing them down and eating off the floor. He then goes out again. Occasionally he will tap on the windows and laughs if anyone looks up. I suggested that he does want to communicate but can only do so if he knows where he is. We introduced a polycarbonate screen. My student put it on her lap and tapped it every time he passed. After a little while he came in and walked all round her looking at her. The second time we came, the screen was on the floor as we tried to explain to the team leader what we were trying to do. He came in at once, picked up the screen, put it on her lap, tapped it and laughed at her.

Another man had withdrawn to his room and carers had great difficulty getting into his room to carry out personal care. He responded to nothing until I started to work with his body language through the glass panel in his door. Immediately he began to laugh and interact. He knew where I was and I no longer seemed to him terrifying and invasive.

A child is able to interact with her teacher when her teacher stands outside the window and presses her nose against the glass. There is a boundary between them that the child can feel.

Children with poor body maps may enjoy playing in boxes or on a swing if they can sit on an adult's lap. These physical boundaries seem to assist in the development of a body map. Deep pressure and weights also help in this process. A child unable to jump can do so when he wears sports weights on his ankles. Another can write when she uses a weighted pencil. Likewise a child with body map problems may be helped by such activities as pushing, pulling, jumping and hanging. These sensations appear meaningful and often produce positive responses.

BALANCE, HEAD MOVEMENTS AND GRAVITY

Information to the brain about balance is provided by the *vestibular system* situated in the inner ear. It tells us if we are moving, how fast we are going and in what direction. It plays a part in our posture. When over-stimulated we feel motion-sick; when under-stimulated we crave movement and may take safety risks in order to gain it.

Children with autism tend to either seek out movement activities or reject them entirely. For some children swinging or spinning does not make them dizzy since they do not actually register such input successfully. Movement in a line such as when sitting in a rocking chair and gently rocking appears to be calming whereas movement of a stop–start variety is alerting and can aid registration. It may help a child who is unresponsive if we constantly change the type of movement so that they get unexpected sensations. For example, we might do some fast swinging followed by winding up and spinning out followed by jiggling from side to side. On the other hand, we might enclose a child who is about to overload on our lap, applying deep pressure whilst gently swinging with movement in a line in one direction only, such as that experienced when sat in a rocking chair.

> A child spends most of his time alone. He will not join in circle time at school but self-stimulates in a variety of ways. He looks out of a small window, framing the view. With his feet still on the ground, using them as a pivot, he swings from curtains, backwards and forwards. On the grounds that his search for a regular movement is purposeful, I suggest that he be taken to trampolining sessions as soon as he comes to school. Since this has been instituted he now comes willingly to join in circle time with the rest of his class.

Generally, the pleasure of a meaningful movement activity can assist the brain in processing other sensory inputs and result in increased eye contact and vocalisations. What the child's brain needs is something it understands.

> Many children with autism have problems *modulating* their vestibular input; that is, knowing how much is enough at any one point on

any one day before they become overexcited and/or overloaded. This difficulty leads to them being unable to increase or reduce the signals from the vestibular system to the central nervous system at that time. It is like having problems with the volume control dial on a radio. The outcome is either that the brain is swamped by signals or they cannot be heard; the dial is on full volume or off. This makes life very difficult on a day-to-day basis.

TASTE AND SMELL

It is embarrassing for a parent and the recipient when a child on the spectrum announces to a woman in a shop, 'You stink!' While this obviously needs to be discouraged, it may also be literally true if the child is hypersensitive to smell. The bath salts this woman used a couple of days ago may smell to him absolutely repulsive so he wants to vomit. A child is distraught when his mother opens the fridge door which has an egg sandwich in it. The smell of egg overwhelms him. If your child is hypersensitive to smell cut out the use of scented toiletries.

The same sort of problems arise with food, although here the difficulty is sometimes with texture – how it feels – rather than taste.

Figure 5.2 A sweet-smelling scent may smell repulsive

SYNAESTHESIA

All this sensory confusion is complicated by a condition known as *synaesthesia*. This is where a particular sensory stimulus is experienced as a different one. For example, taste is sensed as shape. The crossover can happen between any of the senses but remains constant for any pairing. Although it is found in the general population, synaesthesia occurs more frequently among people with autism. (From the point of view of the outsider this always seems bizarre since it threatens our sense of what we know to be real.)

> A woman throws her food on the floor shouting, 'Can't eat that it's too black': she perceives taste as colour.

> A child with Asperger syndrome feels 'cold' as 'wet'. When he gets into a cold bed he thinks he has wet it and gets very upset.

> In her film *Jam-Jar*, Donna Williams talks about soap having a 'very green smell': she perceives smell as colour.[9]

> A woman sees her emotions as colour. Another 'knows' that the days of the week are numbers: 'Monday is one, Tuesday is two and so on.' She is, however, prepared to pander to my perceived error.

We need to try and work out if any of the normal sensory inputs in our lives are upsetting people on the spectrum and try and reduce their incidence.

Key points

- People with autism often experience hypersensitivity (acute over-stimulation from sensory input) or hyposensitivity (under-stimulation from sensory input) through any of the physical senses.

---

9   Williams (1995).

- Often, people with autism also have Irlen syndrome (visual hypersensitivity) and/or hyperacusis (auditory hypersensitivity).
- The essential point to remember is that the level of stress being experienced by your partner directly affects their ability to cope, to respond and to process information. To help prevent your partner from experiencing an autonomic storm, bring down their stress level.
- In order to achieve this, it is helpful to think in terms of a visual and auditory low-arousal environment by reducing overloading stimuli.

6

Emotional Overload

Chapter contents

WARMTH AND AFFECTION

If you want to know what emotional overload feels like, shut your eyes and think of the most embarrassing thing that has ever happened to you. Focus on what it feels like. People will say they feel hot, flushed, tight in the chest, tingling and their heart pounds, all responses

Figure 6.1 A hug may feel painful

triggered by an overactive autonomic nervous system. Now imagine you are hypersensitive to such feelings. This is so unpleasant most people will say they don't even want to think about it. Donna Williams tells us that, in order to avoid it, the body will sometimes cut off from the brain so that the feeling is buried and only triggered later on. Then the body is swept by the tidal wave of feeling. The body's self-defence system is triggered and swept by adrenalin: 'I feel as if I am being attacked, so I respond as if this is so.' (This time lag between the trigger and the response means that links can be missed by ABC charts since there is no direct temporal relationship between the two.)

The feelings that sweep through people as a consequence of emotional overload can lead to dangerous aggression. In someone who is sensitive to this, outbursts can be triggered by any form of emotional warmth, smiles, praise, eye contact, using the person's name, even direct speech. We have to find ways of reducing the stress level.

When I am working with someone who suffers from emotional overload I look over their shoulder rather than at them when I speak. I avoid direct speech, praise, smiles and anything which will arouse emotional warmth. Communication is going to be strictly on their terms.

> A mother tells me she longs to hug her child but when she does so, her daughter bites her. I tell her about Temple Grandin who says that when she was small, she longed to be hugged but when it happened she felt she was being drowned in a tidal wave of unpleasant sensation. Sometimes we may have to love someone so much that we put their need not to be swamped by an emotional response, over and above our need to demonstrate our affection.

PEOPLE AND EYE CONTACT

Then there is the physical difficulty of the sheer amount of processing that people present. If you have autism, it is difficult to hold a shape in your mind. If the shape moves you have to process the shape and the movement. If it makes a sound, all three need processing.

Thérèse Jolliffe tells us that this is why, for her, people are the most difficult of all to process. 'Their shapes constantly move and change and they make complicated sounds which are difficult to understand.'[1]

This leads to the brain cutting off from people. They are just too sensorily demanding. From a practitioner's point of view, when I am working I sometimes feel I am no more to them than a piece of furniture. From my partner's standpoint:

> Ros Blackburn tells her audience that they might as well be a row of chairs.[2]

> A young man says on the audiotape *A Bridge of Voices*, 'I feel like an alien in a foreign world.'[3]

People with emotional overload sometimes may feel more relaxed when there is a physical boundary such as a window between them and other people, because of the sheer amount of sensory stimuli that people present. This is partly because it removes the uncertainty of where the other person starts but also, by lowering the stress level this doubt causes, their brain can more easily process all the other sensations with which it feels it is being bombarded.

Eye contact is especially difficult. Many people on the spectrum have learned to avoid eye contact because it is painful. Instead they may look at the chin or nose or, turning sideways, use their peripheral vision. Alternatively they may wear a cap pulled down over their eyes: not in this case to avoid bright light but to cut down on direct contact with people. Avoiding eye contact does not mean the person is not attending to the speaker – but rather that eye contact hurts.

Thérèse Jolliffe says it is unbearably painful.

Donna Williams says it is agony.

---

1   Jollife *et al.* (1992).

2   Blackburn (2004).

3   Weekes (date unknown).

We who are not autistic are obsessed by eye contact. It is how we judge whether or not we can trust people. Failure to make eye contact leaves us deeply uneasy. We try every way to 'teach' people on the spectrum to 'look at us'.

To insist on eye contact is a form of abuse since it inflicts pain. When we come to using their body language in Intensive Interaction (Chapter 9), we shall find that, as their brain relaxes, people on the autistic spectrum will always give eye contact.

I want to send my partner the message that I understand the rules of their sensory world and that I shall not do anything that causes them pain. I avoid smiles and praise and using their name. For a person who is neurotypical this is not easy and very counter-intuitive – it feels all wrong – but using this approach can make the difference between being able to reach a person and not being able to do so; between triggering an autonomic storm and their remaining calm. If we are trying to engage with people who we suspect are experiencing emotional overload, we may need to:

- avoid eye contact
- avoid smiles
- avoid direct speech
- avoid praise
- avoid emotional warmth.

If we do these things, even if they feel wrong to us, our partner now knows that we understand what it is that gives rise to painful sensations in them and will respond warmly.

> A woman with extremely disturbed behaviour avoided eye contact and frequently attacked those involved in her care. When I avoided eye contact and indirect speech, this woman, who was alleged to dislike strangers, put her arms round me and laid her head on my shoulder.

Key points

- People on the autistic spectrum often have hypersensitive feedback from the autonomic nervous system. The flood of feeling they experience from emotional stimuli is painful to them.
- In trying to avoid or reduce emotional overload, avoid arousing emotional warmth.

7

Confusing Messages

SPEECH

Speech is a minefield for people on the autistic spectrum. It involves so many processes and so much interpretation. Even though some may

Figure 7.1 Speech is hard to understand

understand what is being said to them, such understanding can be at best intermittent and reply may be impossible. Others get a completely scrambled input. In this chapter we shall consider the consequences of such difficulties from a practical point of view.

Understanding and replying

Traditionally it was thought that people on the autistic spectrum who have no (or very limited) speech could be divided into two groups: those who could understand speech but could not organise a reply – and those who were unable even to understand what is said to them. But clinical experience suggests that a better way of looking at this is of a sliding scale. When we use our partner's body language with them and their brain relaxes, we may find that some of those who are thought to be non-verbal are able to understand speech and even sometimes develop the capacity to speak relevantly, within the limits of any learning disability.

> An autistic woman without speech and with no apparent responses to speech – and whose reputation for violent attacks means that she is left alone in her room most of the time – twists her fingers in her hair. I stand by the door and do the same. After a little while I say, 'If I was doing this for some time I should want to brush my hair, and if I wanted to brush my hair, I should put my hairbrush on the bed.' Immediately she seizes her hairbrush from the table by her side and bangs it onto her bed.

It is clear that this woman has understood what is a very complex sentence with dependent clauses. The young man we meet next develops relevant speech even if limited:

> A young man who has no speech has just started attending a day centre. He stands in a corridor and hits anyone who passes by. Periodically he throws chairs and tables. It is not possible to take him out because he randomly attacks members of the public. Using *his* sounds with him, the number of recorded violent incidents reduces from three or four a day, to two in six months. He can now be taken into a busy pub, where he puts his money on the

counter, says 'Coke', goes and sits down and waits quietly for it to be served.

From the outsider's point of view, we are so desperate to get people to speak to us – if only they can talk we shall be able to sort everything out. 'When will they talk?' is one of the commonest questions that parents ask. In our anxiety we try to frogmarch people who cannot speak into our world so we can understand them, without reflecting on what it is that has meaning for their brains. And here we are caught in a paradox. If we always demand that a person uses 'our language', we are increasing their stress level, a situation that underlies some very complex behavioural problems. Where does the balance lie between insisting on 'our-world' communication – and focusing on reducing stress, which allows their brain to function more effectively?

For our partners, just being clever does not necessarily help. In fact it can make the situation worse, because it is assumed by non-autistic partners that there is no problem. Donna Williams, although she speaks four languages, talks about the stress of always trying to interpret speech. She says when she hears one of her own sounds, it's like being thrown a lifebelt in a stormy sea, an image that suggests the stress she experiences from trying to keep up with speech is severe to the point of threatening to trigger the body's self-defence system. 'I run, run, run, always trying to keep up.'[1]

Sometimes it seems, speech is already present in people with ASD but they cannot access it because of the inner turmoil that is going on in their brains. What we see when we use body language as a way of keeping in touch is a visible reduction in stress. Our partner's face muscles relax. Whereas before they have been cut off from their surroundings, they now start to look at them in a more connected and interested way. At this stage it appears that the brain starts to work more effectively and they begin to be able to do such things as generalise, imitate hand movements, use eye contact, seek physical contact and generally relate in ways they have not been able to up until now.

---

1   Williams (1995).

And occasionally they start to use words. The three examples given below are of sessions with non-verbal people with severe autism, the second and third having very severe behavioural disturbances.

> According to his teachers, a child of eight seen at school has no known language. After his first three hours of Intensive Interaction, during which his behaviour moved from withdrawal to engagement, he took the hand of the teacher who came to collect him and clearly said 'Hello'.

> A man of 23 with severe hypersensitivity to sound, who, according to his parents and speech therapist, has only ever been known to say, 'Where's Charlene?' (his sister), had a session of four hours broken by lunch. (The first time Intensive Interaction had been tried with him.) At the end of this he started to sing, 'Baa Baa Black Sheep' loudly and clearly. However, examination of the video of this session shows clearly that he was struggling to show us what he could do some time before he achieved his aim. He got the rhythm first and then the tune and then finally the words – but not before his chin had been wobbling with his effort to articulate the words. He knew what he wanted to do but he really had to work hard to do it.

> After using Intensive Interaction with a non-verbal and very disturbed child of eight (who is extremely hypersensitive to almost everything) for a few months, her mother says the child turned one day to her father and said, 'I love you.' Her speech is now improving rapidly.

We are not claiming that the use of Intensive Interaction will teach children to speak but rather that, by encouraging the brain to relax, it sets up the preconditions for speech, liberating it if the inner language is already present; a situation at least partly dependent on the degree of learning disability.

Fading speech

For the person with autism, interpretation of speech is one of the major problems. It just presents the brain with more stimuli than the processing system can handle.

> An able child (with autism) in school says that sometimes he can hear what the teacher says and sometimes it fades away completely. When it comes back he has absolutely no idea what she has said or is talking about. She says he is naughty because he is not paying attention. He says she doesn't believe him when he tells her what is happening. He gets into trouble and is unhappy to the point of refusing to go to school.

This story is quite common: two realities in conflict because one cannot understand what the other is saying as they do not experience it themselves.

'Words can sound like bullets.'[2]

Thinking and sensing

In her film, *Jam-Jar*, Donna gives us a more refined picture of her thinking, of what happens or rather fails to happen when people speak to her.[3] She says that the sounds don't always make meaning. She tells us how she related to the world outside through a system of 'sensing' (building up an encyclopaedia of sensory experiences). A table was a 'flat, square, brown, thud thing'. She could not move from this list to name it as 'table', nor move on to put it in context, 'the thing you put the plate on'. She says that in a world which constantly demanded interpretation, she was lost and felt totally threatened, especially when told she was being stupid. It was like a war and it was easier to retreat into her own world.

The stress she experiences was brought home to me by an 11-year-old boy with autism.

---

2   Grandin in Arnall and Peters (1992).

3   Williams (1995).

His teacher says he is having a bad morning. He is clearly stressed when I arrive, will not come near me and spends a lot of time flapping his left hand on his nose. I echo the rhythm of his movements by tapping them on a cupboard door. He is disturbed – but manages to say with enormous effort, as though his self is being squeezed through a pinhole, 'Why you doing this?' I am surprised by his speech but reply, 'Because I want to chat to you.' It is as if a bung has been removed. He becomes deeply playful. He takes my head in his hands and gazes into my eyes and puts his head on my lap. His efforts to tell us what is on his mind become more effective. He has previously been saying repetitively, 'Five, four, three, two, one.' Now he goes off and selects a particular video from a pile and fast-forwards it until he comes to a picture of a rocket being launched. What had been repetitive and self-stimulatory becomes something he wants to make clear to us. He is now involved in an interaction in which he takes the initiative to communicate to us what he is thinking.

It is not that people with autism do not want to speak or have nothing to say. Thérèse Jolliffe tells us of the terrible frustration she endured. She says that not being able to organise her reply made her want to scream and hit people and break things.

Clearing the log-jams

Some people get stuck in an early developmental stage and this is reflected in their speech.

A child is still in the stage where he needs his mother (or mother figure) to confirm what he says before he can go on. This child makes sounds but in addition has learned the simple phrases his mother has used with him: 'Put in mouth', 'Put coat on', 'Go in room', etc. But here he comes to a stop and waits for his support partner to repeat these phrases back to him before he can go on and complete the particular activity. If this is not done quickly he becomes extremely upset and attacks her. So far all approaches to help him move forward have failed. I suggest we introduce one of his non-verbal sounds, 'Ahh', before we reply. So at lunch, instead of repeating, 'Put in mouth', we say, 'Aaahh, put in mouth'. Hearing his own sound anchors his attention. We gradually reduce his stereotypic phrase and he can now accept just a nod in acknowledgement. He no longer throws his food at his support partner. Using this technique his relevant speech is improving; for example, he will now say, 'Get in *the* pool', rather than 'Get in pool'.

Another man (this time with Asperger syndrome) is also looking for confirmation so that he can move on. Having been warned that if he started talking about the number nine I should get away as he escalates to the point of lashing out, when I am introduced to him I rather foolishly ask him what he is doing. He replies that he is making meat sandwiches for his supper. Looking at me intently he goes on to ask if I know about the number nine. 'There are number nine buses in the city and 27 is all right because it is three times nine.' He is becoming more and more agitated and has me backed into a corner. I hear myself say, 'Are you going to have nine sandwiches for supper?' He does a double take and laughs and says, 'No, I am going to have three' and goes back to making them. What he needed was a significant answer, one that, in his confused and stuck state, would confirm his fixated utterance and allow him to move on. I used this to redirect his thought pattern back to the world outside his distress.

Non-verbal people may also be looking for confirmation in the form of a message that has significance for their brain, one that in all the turmoil stands out as one they recognise.

A woman hits her mother frequently. I sit near her and make her sounds. Suddenly she stands and hits me, a rain of blows until I let out an involuntary yelp. She stops immediately. Her mother says, 'That's odd, she always stops when she knows she has hurt me.' I get her mother to echo back her sounds to her, answering every one. In the next two days she does not attack her mother once. What she is looking for is a significant response, one that has meaning for her brain.

Some people on the spectrum manage to learn one phrase and use it for everything they want to say. They want to communicate, but this is the only window which they have available.

> A man has only one phrase: 'Go home, get changed, see Dad on Saturday.' Whenever he wants to speak this is all he can say. While he is saying this he becomes very agitated and ends up attacking anyone near him. During lunch he finds he looks round and sees he has no spoon for his yoghurt. He immediately starts on his phrase, 'Go home...', and this escalates. His support partner is trying to answer his phrase logically, 'Today is Friday, Dad is coming tomorrow', but this is not what his disturbance is about. What he is trying to say is, 'I haven't got a spoon to eat my yoghurt.' When he is told to go and fetch a spoon he calms down at once, goes into the kitchen, returns with a spoon and eats his lunch.

If a person has only one catch-all phrase, in order to see what it is that they want we need to look at the current circumstances rather than what they are saying.

Finally:

> A woman who has delayed echolalia (a meaningless repetition of other people's words) can only say, 'It's all right to hold the childer', a phrase she repeats over and over again, sometimes for hours. Trying to engage with this phrase does not get in touch with her – but echoing the rhythm of the phrase offers her brain something it recognises without the complication of the speech. She stops at once and puts her arms round me.

When people are using echolalia, an alternative is to try repeating back the rhythm rather than the words.

Being precise

Sometimes we need to look for a different way of saying what we want so that it gives a clear lead as to what can be expected.

A mother says that her son who has severe autism but is quite verbal cannot answer if he is asked a direct question such as, 'Do you want to go out?' On the other hand he can respond readily if the question is put differently as in, 'Tell me if you want to go out?' He needs to know that he is expected to respond.

Wendy Lawson, who has autism, tells us we never finish our sentences.[4] We say we are going out – but not that we are coming back again. How can we get over such ideas to people who are non-verbal?

I am working with a woman who does not use speech and who gets extremely upset if she is asked to go for a walk. She screams and holds on to the door. I try using gestures to tell her we are going out so that she will understand better but it makes no difference. So next I try pointing at her and myself and then outside at the same time as saying we are going for a walk, followed immediately by pointing to the floor by her feet and saying, 'And then we are coming back again.' She understands completely and no longer protests when she knows she is returning to a place of 'safety', somewhere she knows.

Make sure that your partner knows not only where they are going to go but also where they are coming back to.

Lost voices

Another difficulty that can arise in able people with autism is that they feel so vulnerable that they project parts of themselves outside themselves. What we, the outsider, hear are different voices for 'good Liz' and 'bad Liz'. Good Liz says cheerfully, 'Hello Phoebe, how are you?', and bad Liz says in a growly voice, 'I want to hit Phoebe', because this is how she feels – but has learned that it is unacceptable.[5] Unfortunately the 'bad' bits break out sooner or later in episodes of extreme

---

4   Lawson (2003).

5   For a fuller treatment of the problem of lost voices, see the section 'Lost Voices/Learned Language' in Caldwell with Horwood (2007).

behaviour, either self-harm (to control the unacceptable bits) or aggression.

Think what it is that has meaning for our partner. If we try to engage with the 'learned voices' it is like trying to talk to a mirror image, which has no real substance since it is a projection. In order to reach the 'real person', it is helpful to:

1. confirm and validate their negative feelings (saying we understand how they feel, so in the situation above I say, 'You must feel like hitting Phoebe')

2. use their body language since it speaks to them directly.

Hollow words

It is very misleading when people with autism learn to say words but have no idea of their real meaning. This happens particularly in conjunction with 'time words' such as 'soon', 'later' and 'tomorrow'. These words have no boundaries, nothing to say how long the interval is.

A boy asks his mother, 'When's supper?' Without thinking she says, 'Soon'. He screams at her, 'You know I can't cope with "soon"!' She says 'Six minutes' and he says, 'Right', and goes off to wait.

Because it is so hard for people with autism to process speech, laying too much emphasis on the ability to talk can trigger a high level of stress. I am not trying to suggest that we should abandon our attempts to help people to learn to speak but we do need to be extremely careful about how we go about it. If we lower the stress level we may find that if our partner does not have too great a level of learning disability, speech may emerge by itself.

SIGN AND GESTURE

On the whole I prefer to use clear gestures rather than sign with people on the autistic spectrum, since they find it difficult to deal with anything abstract. I use it not only with non-verbal people but also with some people who are verbal. I do this to reinforce language since some of our partners need a visual as well as an auditory input. I use this particularly if I am working with someone whose behaviour can be dangerous, I also wait for a response indicating they have understood. This may be as little as a flick of the eyes – but I need to make absolutely sure that they understand what I am going to do before I do it.

One idea at a time

It is important to present only one idea at once.

> A boy who is very easily tipped into aggressive behaviour can manage to indicate what he wants to do through a picture board at the beginning of or end of a task. However, if for any reason he is presented with a choice in the middle of a task (for example his teacher might feel he needs to go to the toilet or is becoming upset and would prefer some time out), this throws him completely and he attacks the nearest person. He cannot cope with more than one train of thought at a time. If presented with more, he tips immediately into an autonomic storm.

It is very important that other people do not have conversations 'over the top' of their partner because they simply cannot sort out the confusion in their brain.

ABSTRACT IDEAS

If it is difficult to hold a shape in the mind, how much harder is it to hold on to an idea which has no shape to recommend it, nothing to latch on to? Even if the person has speech, time is a big problem, because 'intervals' are hard to grasp. They may be able to say 'later' or 'next week' but have no idea how long this is. We have already met the boy who screams at his mother if she says 'Soon' but is quite happy to wait when she changes it to six minutes. Try and be precise and latch the time of the event on to part of their familiar routine. For example say, 'Two sleeps' instead of 'The day after tomorrow'. Our partners need to know what is happening, when it will happen and who will be around when it happens.

The same problem is still there if our partner has no speech and we still need to find ways of making intervals easier to understand.

> A young man, who has Down's syndrome as well as autism, goes home from day centre and has to wait two hours until the taxi comes to take him to his music lesson, which he loves. He knows that it will come but has no idea how long two hours is and becomes more and more worked up as time passes. We give him a jar, eight wooden balls and a 15-minute egg timer. Each time the bell rings he can put a ball in the jar. He likes doing this. It is fun dropping the ball into the jar when the bell rings. It does not matter that he cannot count, all he needs to grasp is that all the balls need to be in the jar before it is time to go.

Timetables and clocks

Visual timetables help but many of the ones we currently offer our partners can be visually very confusing. For example, our partner may not understand that he has to move from left to right in order to follow a week. We need to design simple clocks and timetables. The whole point of these very simple timepieces is that they are designed to make it easy to distinguish between 'now' and 'not now'.

What makes telling the time difficult (or rather getting over the idea of when something is going to happen) is having two hands. We can make a simple clock with one hand.

Buy the works of an electric clock and a pair of hands (preferably straight kitchen-clock hands). The works now come in a pack, about the size of a cigarette pack, and can be obtained through a watchmaker. The pack has a spindle to hold the hands in its centre. Choose a suitable piece of white board and drill a hole for the spindle through the centre. Insert the spindle.

For a twelve-hour clock, throw away the minute hand and mount the hour hand. For an hour clock, throw away the hour hand and mount the minute hand.

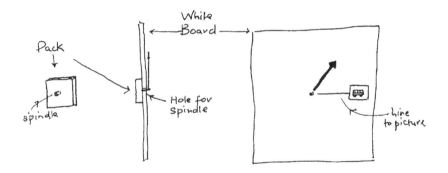

Figure 7.2 Day clock/hour clock

Do not put figures or black velcro on the face since these are visually distracting. Instead of figures, use pictures of the intended activity, starting with just one picture so that it is visually simple. Draw a line from the centre of the clock to the picture.

If you need to be able to use alternative pictures to swap in and out according to the day's activities, mount them on card, laminate them and use white self-adhesive velcro to stick them to the board.

Day timetable

Stick a strip of velcro long enough to take flash cards of all the partner's daily activities on a length of ply about 70cm long. Use laminated flash cards with a picture of the activity on one side, and dark Fablon (sticky-backed plastic) on the back. Attach these to the board by a small patch of velcro on front – and one on the back so they can be turned over.

For example, a list of daily activities at a day centre might run like this: 'Taxi, Tea, Shopping, Tea, Cooking, Lunch, Tea, Activity, Tea, Taxi', which gives us ten flash cards. These are turned over before the change of activity. The rest remain face to the board, so our partner can always refer to his timetable to see what he is meant to be doing at any particular moment.

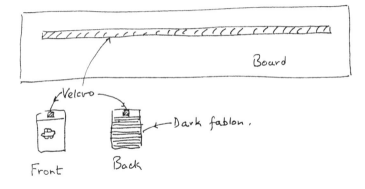

Board

Velcro

Dark fablon.

Front   Back

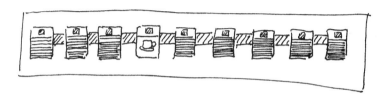

Figure 7.3 Day timetable: picture on front of card, Fablon on back; velcro on both sides so the card can be turned over

Week timetable

We need a strip of batten with seven cup hooks on it, one for each day of the week. A strip of ply, with a strip of velcro down the centre, hangs from each hook.

On each day we can place flash cards with either a photograph of the person who is their supporter today, or the main activities for the day. The point of being able to take each day off the hook is that holding it alone in one hand makes it easy to separate the days, so that one can say, for example, 'Look, this one is Tuesday' and take another off, hold it in the other hand and say, 'This one is today, and today is Thursday.' The physical separation helps to make it easier to understand.

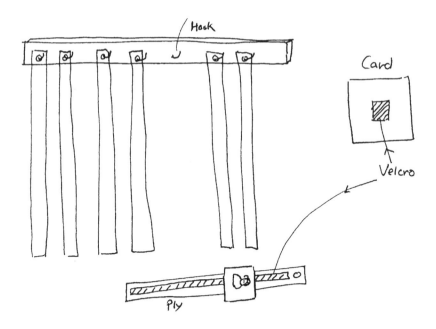

Figure 7.4 Week timetable

Year timetable

To make a year timetable, use an office calendar. Looked at as a whole, it is not clear which way to go on this calendar, so cut the months into separate strips and mount on a dark background. Cross off one day at a time and mark special days with a picture, for example a Christmas tree for Christmas.

CHOICES AND CHANGE

The problem with both choices and change is that they require a sudden heavy load of processing.

Choices

In order to give people some control over their lives we feel we should help people to learn to make choices, so that they can have what they want rather than what we think they ought to have. However, for some

Figure 7.5 Year timetable (made from office calendar)

people on the autistic spectrum this can present an intolerable process-ing burden. We need to be flexible. The people who find choices impossible will tip into fragmentation and aggression immediately they are offered a choice. In this case, rather than offering the alterna-tives simultaneously we need to offer them one by one. 'Will you have this?' and if it is rejected, 'Will you have this one?'

Change

Changes in programmes are notorious for upsetting people – but it is difficult for us to avoid them in real life. Our partners have just about got hold of the idea of what is going to happen and are clinging to this, when suddenly they are being told something different is going to happen. It sets off all sorts of conflicting messages in the brain.

We need to try and help our partners know what is happening. Some people (those who can decipher what is on a flash card) are helped by a 'change board' (see Figure 7.6). This board uses flash card to support the necessity of change.

In sequence, left to right, this board has:

1. a cup hook for flash cards with pictures of the intended activity (1a). When the activity has to be changed, this is covered by a 'change card' with a picture of the reason for change (1b)

2. a picture of our partner

3. an arrow

4. a flash card with a picture of the alternative activity.

Suppose the intended activity is swimming but the taxi has broken down. The proposed alternative is cooking. Flash card (1a) shows swimming. The transport has failed so (1a) is covered by change card (1b) which shows a picture of a flat tyre.

Reading the board from left to right we now have the sequence: the taxi is not coming (flash card), 'you' (picture), go to (arrow), cooking (flash card).

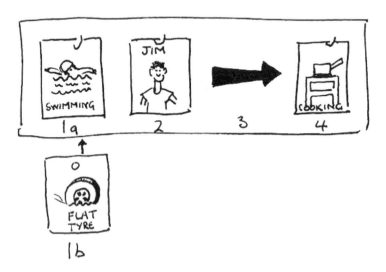

Figure 7.6 Change board

At least we now have a way to negotiate, something concrete we can refer to instead of relying on the wobbly foundation of speech, which when a person is stressed simply adds to their confusion. (Although I have not personally tried this, it should at least in theory be possible to use sequential *objects of reference*[6] instead of flash cards, if necessary.)

While we cannot expect all the above suggestions to work with any particular partner, all of them have already helped someone – and are therefore worth consideration. What is most important is to reduce the sensory clutter that overloads our partner's brain and introduce meaningful signals so that they can work out what is going on round them. In the next chapter we are going to consider a sensory day in the life of a hypothetical child and then, in Chapter 9, look at exactly how it is we go about using body language to communicate with our partners.

Key points

- There are so many aspects to spoken language that require processing. Speech can therefore pose difficulty for people on the autistic spectrum to varying degrees.
- However, if a person on the autistic spectrum is non-verbal, it does not necessarily mean they are unable to understand speech. If the stress the brain experiences can be reduced they may start to use appropriate speech, depending on the level of learning disability.
- We need to reduce the amount of information that requires processing when we communicate with our partners and give clear messages.
- Confusing messages can sometimes be made more concrete through the use of visual clues.

---

6 Objects of reference are objects that relate directly to an activity and help our partner to know what they are doing. For example, a towel for swimming, soap for a bath, car keys for a drive, and so on. They are not the same as signs, which may be too abstract for a person on the severe end of the spectrum.

8

Case Study: A Day in the Life of Mike

Chapter contents

A NORMAL DAY IN THE LIFE OF MIKE

We live in a real world. So let us start a normal school-day in the life of a hypothetical child on the autistic spectrum and see what sensory distress he may be encountering.

Mike wakes up. He has had a bad night because his sleep pattern is disturbed. He is light sensitive so drawing the curtains hurts his eyes. He prefers to keep his room in darkness. Brushing his hair and teeth is a problem because his skin is acutely painful. The telephone rings and the bell sound hurts his ears.

Mike knows the bus is coming to take him to school but waiting is a problem. He has two conflicting messages circling round his brain: 'The bus is coming' and 'The bus isn't here'. Trying to sort this out is upsetting him.

The journey to school from one place to another is really hard. There is so much processing of different images to work through. His brain is swimming with 'interference'. Today there are road works so the bus is diverted down unfamiliar streets. This is too much and Mike starts to hit himself. Getting out of the bus he loses track of his feet. He is still in fragmentation when he arrives at school.

Mike goes to a reasonably good school but the environment presents an overwhelming avalanche of sensory stimuli – lots of people moving around, the noise of speech, assembly in a large echoing hall, even the school uniform which is a cheerful red. The walls are covered with children's work. Everything is designed to be stimulating.

Mike's day starts with circle time when all the children in his class are welcomed. This is designed to help the children feel part of the group and make them aware of the other children in their class. Unfortunately Mike has problems with proximity and cannot cope with sitting close to the other children. The noise hurts him. He tries to escape but the bolt on the door is high up beyond his reach. He sits in the corner as far as possible from the group and rocks. If he focuses on this movement he may just be able to hold himself together.

Circle time is over. His teacher collects Mike, still protesting, and takes him to his workstation. Mike's highly structured programme provides some sensory respite. In his workstation the routine is familiar and Mike knows what he is doing, but the strip lighting hurts his eyes and the light bounces off the white surface of his table. He does his tasks mechanically – he knows what he has to do but is not really interested or motivated to explore.

For Mike, break time is a nightmare. (Listen to children in a playground. A random shouting, shoving swirl of unpredictable noises and movements – a boy in *A is for Autism*[1] says 'I thought I was going to go mad', so he stood and concentrated on flapping his hand.) Mary brushes against Mike. It feels like an assault. He does not know where up or down are. He is afraid, screams and lashes out. Similarly, lunch in the hall is a horrific sensory assault and he bolts for the door.

Oh yes, and Mike is ten and just coming into puberty. On top of all the other sensory problems he experiences, not only is he generally

---

1   Child in Arnall and Peters (1992).

more sensitive to those sensory inputs that used to hurt him but he is also occasionally overwhelmed by tidal waves of unpleasant sensation which appear to come without warning and over which he has no control.

And so on through the day. When he gets home his mother is told he has been excluded from the bus because he hit Jim and he is naughty. By the time she manages to get Mike upstairs to his bedroom, Mike's mother is totally exhausted and dreading the negotiations with the authority she will have to start tomorrow to get a taxi provided.

Because we do not experience the same level of sensory distress as Mike, we only see his behaviour which we judge to be aggressive and difficult to manage.

Such is the diversity in autism that to some parents and teachers with a child who has been diagnosed as being on the spectrum this may seem an exaggeration. But others will recognise the pattern of a daily struggle to even begin to contain a child who is clearly in extreme sensory distress, which is very often being misread as 'difficult' and 'challenging'.

A BETTER DAY FOR MIKE

Maybe we should do a sensory re-run for Mike.

Mike wakes and the curtains remain drawn. He has a dimmer light switch by his bed so that he can control the level of lighting. He uses a mouthwash to clean his teeth and his mother has had the telephone ring tone changed to a frequency that does not hurt his ears. She uses the special one-handed clock to let him know when the taxi is coming for him.

When Mike reaches school, he does not go into assembly but is taken in through a side door. On the basis that Mike calms himself by rocking (which provides a recognisable jerk to his vestibular system), his first activity is a session on the trampoline to calm him down by offering his brain a stimulus that has meaning. From here he is taken to his workstation. This has been repainted a neutral colour and has a clip-on light with the colour that helps him process information. At break he wears a cap to cut down the light and a gilet with weights in the pockets so that he can focus on these instead of the swirling sensory turmoil around him. He has lunch in a quiet room.

What we are doing is modifying Mike's environment, so that he is not constantly being subjected to overload by stimuli to which he is hypersensitive and which cause him pain. But at this stage, the question we need to answer is, how far can we modify Mike's environment to provide a user-friendly world, instead of one that Thérèse Jolliffe describes as offering 'a life of terror'?[2]

Given that we cannot always eliminate the sensory confusion Mike is going to experience, is there any other way we can help to provide a stable and coherent picture of the world for this child? In the next chapter we are going to look at using body language to help Mike and the children (and adults) like him to make more sense of the world and relate to the people in it. It is like using a smart card to gain access; you need to use the correct code.

> **Key points**
> - Ask the questions: which factors/activities help the individual to be calm, and which cause distress?
> - Consider how you can make use of the kinds of sensory input that have a calming, regulating effect on your partner.

---

2   Jolliffe, Lansdown and Robinson (1992)

9

Intensive Interaction

In the Introduction we discussed the two ideas underlying Intensive Interaction: first, the infant–mother imitation conversations where the infant initiates, mother confirms and baby moves on to something new; and second, the mirror neuron system.

Deep down, this way of communicating with each other remains with us as a process all our lives. If I see someone else doing something, it fires off the same network of neurons in my brain as would be triggered if I was doing it myself. In a literal sense, I feel what you are doing. The mirror neurons in our brain recognise and latch on to this extremely quickly. Although it is suggested that in people with autism this network may not be working normally, observation of many people on the autistic spectrum suggests that they do always recognise a gesture if it is part of their own body language. So even if we have autism, our mirror neuron system does recognise our partner's initiatives provided they are part of our normal repertoire.

USING OUR BODY LANGUAGE TO COMMUNICATE

We start with observation. What is our partner doing? People on the autistic spectrum find words and conversation so confusing that they turn in on themselves and listen to their own brain–body language. If I want to join in and talk to you, I am going to have to look at what you are doing and use your gestures or sounds or movements, the feedback you are giving yourself, to build up a conversation with you.

This does not mean that I regard you as infantile but rather that I value the way that you talk to yourself so much that I will learn your private language in order to be able to communicate with you. This also says I value you for yourself, not as I think you ought to be.

A young man with autism flicks objects. When he is upset he bellows and beats his head against the wall. His psychologist says that all attempts to communicate with him have failed. He will not let anyone sit near him. Using a similar piece of string I sit on the floor near him and flick my string. At first he grabs mine but becomes progressively more tolerant of my presence, moving from interest in what I am doing to interest in me as a person, responding with shy smiles and eye contact. Eventually he is examining my face extremely closely, introducing new activities and referring back to me to see what I make of this.

A child is lost in an inner world. He grunts and scratches his fingers. I sit near him and scratch my own, taking care that they are in a position where he can see what I am doing. Every time he grunts, I answer him. After a little while he looks at me, smiles and puts out his hand to hold mine. Now, every time he makes a sound, I 'draw' the sound on his arm, different shapes that echo the 'shape' of the sound he is making. He laughs.

A man who is non-responsive and frequently aggressive cannot bear touch on his body. He licks his lips, round and round and round. I draw the circular movement on his foot. He smiles and then breaks out laughing when I reverse the direction of the movement. We have shared a joke.[1]

A boy on the spectrum who has no speech and is known to have violent outbursts gets some earth in his mouth. I have been using his sounds with him for an hour or so. While his teacher fetches a drink, I make a face as if I also have earth in my mouth and pretend to spit it out. He looks at me, laughs, and does the same. Again, we have shared a joke using facial language.

Some people are caught in a closed loop of behaviour which cuts them off from other people and their surroundings. In effect, they are talking to themselves: their brain is giving them the same signals over and over again, a message which they do not find threatening. In all these situations I have observed what my partner is doing (how their brain and body are talking to each other) and joined in. I need to let them know that if they make a movement or sound, I will respond in a non-stressful way that has meaning for their brain.

LOOKING FOR SIGNIFICANT FEEDBACK

We need to look out for the feedback our partners are giving themselves: what is it that they are focusing on in order to know what is happening, to maintain coherence?

1. Observation: What *exactly* is our partner doing in a physical sense? (This is not the same as what we think they *ought* to be doing.)

   Are they using the following?:

   ○ visual feedback
     – poking eyes
     – flapping fingers

---

1   A wider range of case histories form the main focus of Caldwell (2000, 2004, 2005; Caldwell with Horwood 2007). There is also a training video demonstrating the use of Intensive Interaction (Caldwell 2003).

- flapping objects
- spinning objects
- flashing objects
- watching shadows move

o auditory feedback
- tapping
- making small sounds in the throat
- hitting objects
- bellowing
- screaming

o tactile feedback
- stroking – themselves or an object
- scratching – themselves or elsewhere

o proprioceptive stimulus
- banging or hitting themselves
- applying pressure
- jumping
- walking in circles

Figure 9.1 This man bangs his head in an attempt to maintain coherence when he is starting to go into an autonomic storm

- − trampolining
- − swinging
- − rocking

    ○ fixating on an external stimulus or theme 'hijacked' from the world outside themselves
  - − tearing paper
  - − shutting doors
  - − drawing cats
  - − counting
  - − watching a particular video or DVD
  - − cars
  - − trains
  - − computers.

2. As well as looking and listening to what our partner is doing, we also observe how they are doing it. What does it tell us about how they are feeling? Are we picking up any of that feeling in ourselves?

3. In order to join their conversation, we reflect back to them the signals with which they are familiar. They usually stop and listen, because they are surprised. 'That's my signal but where did it come from?' So they look round to see. When it is repeated, they usually respond. We are trying to move them from solitary occupation to an activity we can share.

This kind of intervention is more than just copying and needs to be thought of as a way of developing conversation, with all the skills that we use when we are talking to each other. We take turns, listen and respond, giving each other space, and adding new and related material. At first we may do this by mirroring, doing the same things to ourselves, or joining in, doing the same thing with them. For example, even if someone is banging themselves, we might echo their banging by tapping ourselves or the door or, if they will tolerate it, go on to tapping them very lightly, using the same rhythm.

On the other hand, using Intensive Interaction is not just about crisis management. Our partner may be listening to something as simple as the noise made by sucking their tongue or sounds in the throat. Always work off what is happening at the present time, not what was effective yesterday or even ten minutes ago or worked for someone else.

ADDING VARIATION

One of the mistakes people make when they start using Intensive Interaction is to think of it in terms of just 'copying' what their partners are doing. We do not always mimic or copy or imitate – but rather watch to see how our 'conversation' grows. Interventions and responses will be modified as our exchange proceeds. We notice if they try out something new and answer this – and we also introduce variations ourselves.

But these need to be variations which do not stray too far, having something in common with the original or with some other element of their body language. For example we may try a movement another way round or answer a sound with touch. (It is like jazz, where we may extemporise – but always in relation to the original theme.) We may also change the way that an activity is done. The important point is that every time our partner does something they learn they will get a significant answer.

We can add variation by:

- altering the timing, pitch or shape of a sound – changing the rhythm or introducing suspense

- altering the mode – beating the rhythm of a person's rocking on the arm of a chair or scraping it on a length of corrugated tube

- bringing in a discontinuity in expectation:

  o We can bring in different but related material. For example, a man likes dogs. We look at pictures of dogs. He smiles when I bark as we look at each new picture. When his brain has got used to the idea that I will do this, the next dog picture I miaow like a cat and he falls about laughing.

○ Or we can leave out something the brain is expecting. For example, a woman walks in front of me, banging her feet on the pavement. I bang mine. When I am sure she is listening, I miss out one of my 'bangs'. She swings round at once laughing.

We need to be creative in the context of what has significance for our partner's brain.

It is vital that we pick up our partner's new initiatives. In doing so we are giving the person the message that we are interested in what they are saying. If we miss these, we are telling them we are not listening to them. We need to convey to them that we value what they do, the language they are using to talk to themselves and, by implication, who they are.

Problems can arise if no variety is introduced, either by us or by them.

A woman who rocks is interested when her partner first rocks with her but gradually becomes less so to the point where her partner feels she is no longer part of a conversation but is being used to feed the woman's need. Interactivity has been lost.

In fact it is the element of surprise that has gone missing – it is surprise that keeps the process open-ended. When this happens, our partner's brain may *habituate*: we begin to feel we are being 'used' as an object – we have been built in to the closed loop of their stereotypic world.

Timing is very important. We must respond to what they are doing now and it should never be mechanical. (This is why recording their sounds and playing them back is rarely successful. They sometimes are briefly attracted and then lose interest. It needs to be a personal response to the present.) We should feel we are talking to friends, giving them time to reflect on what is happening.

Some people worry that using a person's repetitive behaviour to 'talk' to them will increase their fixation on it, reinforcing their stereotypic behaviour. In practice this does not happen. We are shifting our partner's attention away from the perseverant message of the brain–body language to engagement with the world outside.

If the person begins to show signs of distress or overload, we need to return to the original pattern or shorten the time of the intervention. This can happen occasionally with people with autism – they find the excitement too much. Very occasionally, it will trigger a seizure in people with epilepsy. If this should happen we need to shorten the time of the intervention and be extremely careful never to 'hype up' our partner, to raise the level of excitement. Our aim should always be to centre them. Provided we are working sensitively with a person's own language and responding to how we feel they feel, our partner normally becomes relaxed and enjoys the intervention.

Sometimes people need to rest. They appear to withdraw. We need to wait while they take in their new experiences. If they are interested they will come back for more when they are ready.

Most stereotypical and repetitive behaviours can be helped by entering in to them, exploring them and working with them creatively. We need to observe our partners as they are and be non-judgemental about them. In particular we should not dismiss their activities as having no value for communication just because they are simple and not in accord with what we feel is interesting and worthy of our attention, such as clicking or blowing raspberries. We should join in even if we do not feel such activities will help us to get close. We are trying to let people know that there is a world outside their closed stereotype with which they can communicate through their own language and help them to enjoy getting in touch. Apart from shared pleasure during the session, the usual outcome is an increase in confidence. By using the stimuli that our partner's brain recognises (but does not have to put through the processing system) it is as if we are putting stepping stones into the river of unprocessed stimuli, showing our partner where it is safe to go.

WHEN AND FOR HOW LONG SHOULD WE INTERACT?

We need to be practical. Schools will probably allocate time for sessions. On the whole, I want to use body language as part of the total communication system, in the same way as we use our spoken language to engage our partner's attention as often as possible. Perhaps they are tapping, so I tap something each time I pass them. If all the people who support them do this, they get a constant drip-feed of user-friendly messages from the world outside their inner enclave. Each time they get a significant input, however small, it draws their attention to the world outside their inner world.

And we also must not forget to use our communication to have fun with each other. Most of us will be familiar with the fun we can have when we discover a common bond with a friend.

As a language it can be used bilingually, so, for example, we may use a person's sounds to 'gift-wrap' a message which contains a message they would otherwise find difficult.

> A man with autism is upset when he is told he is going to have a bath. We use his sounds to contain the message, holding his attention in a positive way so that he does not feel threatened: 'Ah-ah, Martin, bath, ah-ah.'

As we become more proficient in the use of their language, we may be able to use it to help our partners when they are becoming distressed, by entering in to their world and by using it to draw their attention to the outside world.

> If a person is banging their head on the wall and we bang the same rhythm, it is usually enough to get them to look up: it interrupts the internal message loop. When they look up I knock the wall again but at the same time use my facial language to indicate a question (raised eye-brows and head to one side): 'Is this what we are doing now?' (It is interesting that they do seem to recognise facial language when their attention is focused on an exchange with the world outside.) When they repeat their banging I gradually infiltrate the rhythm of their sounds and

introduce variations. Almost always this becomes an exchange as they realise that each time they do something they will get a response. Their attention shifts to engagement as they become progressively more interested in the quality of my response to their initiatives and refer back to me to see what I will make of it and what I will do next.

So I will engage even with their biting and head banging.

Figure 9.2 Interacting with people who are self-harming

People sometimes say they feel silly trying to mirror activities they may see as infantile. When this happens it is because we are thinking about ourselves rather than our partners.

First of all we are not exactly mirroring: we are using elements of their language to respond to them. It is crucial that we recognise that using the way they talk may be the *only* way we can get in touch with them. We have to put aside our own blueprints of what is 'normal' for us and enter a world that our partner recognises as non-threatening and acceptable. Flicking a bead on a string may not seem an important activity to us, although we ourselves may be surprised what we learn about our partner's sensory world once we start to share it. The activity may not be important in itself but our sharing is critical. If we do this, we will find we are able to relate in a way that we never have before. It is common for people who are working in this way to say they feel quite differently about those they work with, no longer as people they have to bring up or look after but as friends whose company they take pleasure in.

Particularly it is important to remember that Intensive Interaction is not something we *do to* our partners but something we *share with* them, listening and responding to each other. It is very easy to fall into the role of entertainer, teacher or carer instead of equal. We are looking for dialogue rather than monologue.

And we may also use the approaches offered by Sensory Integration, providing opportunities to enhance proprioceptive input through the use of weights such as sports weights (currently obtainable from Argos and Tesco's, among other stores) sewn into a gilet or jacket, or placed round the ankles or wrists. A backpack filled with heavy books can provide weight when going out and in the playground.

Children and adults can be offered 'weight-bearing activities' that involve pushing, pulling, carrying, lifting and tugging; for example, digging, pushing a wheelbarrow or shopping trolley or case on wheels, playing tug-of-war or carrying heavy books from one class room to another. Young adults can benefit from the use of free-weights and resistive gym equipment within an exercise programme on a regular basis. Such simple strategies can help our partner by giving them an outlet to focus on rather than the turmoil inside.[2]

Further, once we have got our partner 'listening' and attending, it is important to give them control. In order to build confidence they need to know that what they do affects what we will do. This is the basis of communication.

Using a person's body language with them (and where appropriate, the techniques of Sensory Integration) can focus attention so powerfully that the brain becomes selective and can filter out the triggers to hypersensitivity; now they have a point of reference, interest in this can override the overload.

> A young man with extremely severe autism is hypersensitive to the whine of planes passing overhead. Each time one passes, his eyes roll up to the left. On video one can see that after 20 minutes using his sounds and movements to communicate he is no longer disturbed by the high-frequency sound.

It is important that a number of supporters share the interventions rather than just one person doing them. In the latter case, our partner may become fixated on 'their' partner. Interaction needs to be a team activity. Sometimes our partner will enjoy sharing a conversation with a number of partners at the same time, looking from one to the next and inviting responses from them in turn.

---

2   Jane Horwood has written two very helpful pamphlets on using Sensory Integration with children: *How to Become a Sensory Detective* (2006) and *Activities to Promote Sensory Integration in Children* (2004).

Key points

- People on the autistic spectrum have difficulty with spoken conversations. In order to communicate with them in a way that they will find much less stressful, we can use *their own* language instead: their body language.
- Intensive Interaction is not about straightforward mimicry of our partner. We need to add variation to the communication, making sure that we don't deviate too far from how we have been communicating, in order to develop the conversation.
- Intensive Interaction is not something we do to our partner, it is a way of being with them.

10

So What about Distressed Behaviour?

Chapter contents

EXTREME DISTRESS

Talking to parent groups, the question that dominates the minds of some parents is often expressed as, 'Yes, this is all very well, but he seems to go berserk sometimes. What do I do when he screams, spits, bites, hits himself and attacks me?'

What we have to remember is that, if a child or adult is showing distressed and disturbed behaviour, it is because they are sensorily overloaded in one way or another. They are far too busy trying to deal with this for it to be anything other than a desperate cry for help. The first thing we have to do is to reduce the sensory input they are experiencing.

INTERVENTIONS WITH PEOPLE IN CRISIS

- Wear drab-coloured clothing.

- Use minimum speech since this adds to sensory input which has to be processed. If you do speak, speak softly (sometimes you may need to whisper).

- Listen before entering your partner's room. Are there any sounds? If so, respond so that you have their attention before you go in. If possible, do not cross the threshold until you have already established contact – even if the key worker has gone straight in and is telling the partner to 'Say hello'. Ideally we need to introduce ourselves in their language before we enter their space, so that when we do come closer we do not present ourselves as threatening to overload them.

- Use gesture (pointing) to ask if you may come in. Remember that your partner is in crisis and wait for a body language response, even if it is only a flicker of the eyelids or sideways glance or grunt. If there is no response or a negative one, wait and try again. You are trying to give them control so that they will know that you are not going to do something that frightens them.

- If your partner responds 'Yes', move only over the threshold and then stop. Wait for them to assemble a picture of you. Then say, 'May I sit down?' and indicate a chair.

- Look and listen to what your partner is doing. Start to do it with them. Watch their response before you try again. Give them time to respond.

- Always get permission before introducing something new. Make sure they know what you are going to do before you do it.

- Try not to ask them to do something when they are in the middle of doing something else.

- If they are avoiding eye contact, do the same. Look over their shoulder when addressing them to reassure them you understand their rules and are not going to do something that will cause pain.

- Look for the feedback the person is giving themselves. In addition look for what disturbs them (hypersensitivities – visual disturbances – can arise from intensity of light, colour and pattern; not knowing what is happening; emotional overload; speech; anything abstract; change; choices; and hormonal surges particularly in puberty). Also what calms them (visual and auditory tranquillity, weights to focus on and Intensive Interaction).

- Reduce the disturbing factors if possible. Put in significant stimuli for them to focus on.

- If our partners are verbal, watch out for 'learned phrases' and 'different voices' expressing negative feelings. Tune into negative feelings by using the dominant word with empathy, for example, 'You must feel you want to hit me', or, 'You must feel pissed off.'

- If our partner is in crisis use their body language with them but give them plenty of space, standing as far away as is possible while still holding their attention.

- If they appear to be irritated by your presence or intervention, back away, open your arms, put your head on one side, raise your eye-brows. While acknowledging your partner's rejection of your intervention, the question you are asking with your body language is, 'Is this better?' You are telling them that you recognise that they feel threatened and accept it. At the same time you are valuing how they feel without breaking off contact. (It is extremely rare to be attacked while using a person's body language. Of the hundreds of people whom I have partnered, only two have ever attacked me, even though many have been highly disturbed. Once was because I made a mistake in timing and tried to get too close, too quickly. On the whole our partner's brain is so fascinated by our interaction that attention is shifted away from the turmoil that is going on in the brain to a recognisable signal: it's like iron filings to a magnet.)

- It may be difficult to believe but once you try this you will find that your partner's difficult to manage behaviour is quickly reduced and often disappears altogether.

- When you find a successful way of interaction, do not discontinue this just because your partner got better. You have modified the environment, rather than cured the autism. The brain will still need to hear or see the familiar points of reference to keep your partner on course: like putting cat's eyes in the road, one after another, letting the motorist know where it is safe to drive.

- Remember, we are trying to introduce an autism-friendly environment in order to lower the stress level (see Figure 10.1).

Key points

- Distressed behaviour is the result of sensory overload.
- Reduce the amount of sensory information that the individual with autism needs to take in and process.
- Use a mode of communication that is based on the individual's own body language. Pay close attention to their behaviour and to *how they respond to your responses*. Adapt your behaviour accordingly, constantly monitoring its effect.
- When you find a way of interacting that works, don't stop using it just because your partner is now doing better. Intensive Interaction and Sensory Integration are not cures for autism – they are radical ways of providing an environment that helps to make sense for our autistic partner.

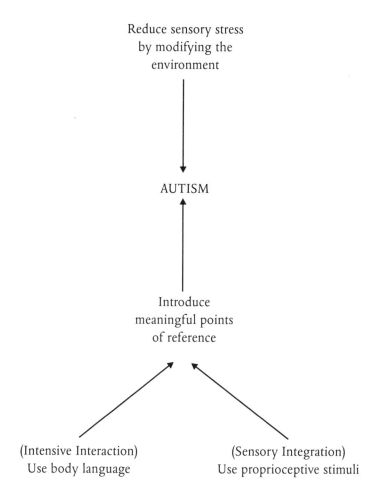

Figure 10.1 The autism-friendly environment

11

Conclusion

In this book we have adopted an approach which combines a reduction in sensory stress through a low-arousal environment, *together* with the introduction of significant and consistent messaging. These significant inputs we are using are derived:

1. from our partner's own body language

2. where suitable, through the use of powerful physical stimuli on which the brain can focus.

Both aim to help our partner maintain coherence so that in the middle of sensory confusion they begin to make sense of what is going on.

In addition to helping to provide a meaningful environment, Intensive Interaction is about establishing relationships, developing emotional engagement and getting to know another person in a way that lets them know how much we value them as they are (without triggering the overwhelming internal feelings that can be so painful) and also offers them a way to express how they feel. As expressed in Figure 10.1, we do this by paying attention to (and trying to reduce) those aspects of their lives which cause them distress – and also by providing a consistent input of sensory signals that hold our partner's attention to a world outside themselves, presenting it as an autism-friendly environment. Apart from using our body language to achieve this, it may also be helpful to use weights or physical activities on which they can focus their attention.

The quality of our exchange is one of shared intimacy, where what matters is being with rather than what we do. With an attitude of profound respect we enter a partnership with another person who is not us, where we are totally tuned in to our partner, where all our attention is given to the minute and intimate affective flickers in their changing body language. At its most profound moments, we enter the dyadic state familiar to infant–mother bonding, the flow where we are aware of both self-and-other, where we are simultaneously 'I' and 'we'.

Of course we cannot stay on these heights, but we will find that having shared these experiences, we have a better understanding of our partner's sensory world and, as they always have meaningful points of reference to which they can anchor themselves, they begin to lead calmer lives. As for us, we have been inside and looked out from their point of view. We have learned to walk in their shoes and it an experience that changes both our lives. Meanwhile, if our partners make sounds, answer them softly. It may be the first time in their lives they have heard something their brain can make sense of. It will provide a safe path, one that in practical terms leads them away from the autonomic storms that so terrify them. Once the brain is no longer under siege, it is able to work more effectively and respond to the world outside, both in emotional and functional terms. Now we can meet and enjoy each other's company.

Bibliography and Useful Resources

BY PROFESSIONALS

Ayres, A.J. (1979) *Sensory Integration and the Child*. Los Angeles, CA: Western Psychological Services.

Blairs, S. and Slater, S. (2007) 'The clinical application of deep touch therapy with a man with autism presenting with severe anxiety and challenging behaviour.' *British Journal of Learning Disabilities 35*, 214–220.

Caldwell, P. (n.d.) *CAN WE TALK? Getting in Touch with People with Severe Learning Disabilities who have Little or No Speech – and Whose Disability is Linked to Autistic Spectrum Disorder (ASD): A Handbook for Families and Carers*. Available online at www.nwtdt.com/Archive/pdfs/Can%20we%20talk%20(Revised).pdf. Accessed 6 December 2007. (Very simple free handout on autism and Intensive Interaction.)

Caldwell, P. (n.d.) *SPEAK TO ME! A Simple Guide to Using Intensive Interaction to Get in Touch with Nonverbal Children and Adults who have Severe Learning Difficulties and/or Autism*. Available online at www.nwtdt.com/pdfs/SPEAK%20TO%20ME.pdf. Accessed 6 December 2007. (Very simple free handout on autism and Intensive Interaction.)

Caldwell, P. (2000) *You Don't Know What it's Like: Finding Ways of Building Relationships with People with Severe Learning Disabilities, Autistic Spectrum Disorder and Other Impairments*. Brighton: Pavilion.

Caldwell, P. (2003) *Learning the Language: Building Relationships with People with Severe Learning Disability, Autistic Spectrum Disorder and Other Challenging Behaviours*. Brighton: Pavilion. (Training video.)

Caldwell, P. (2004) *Crossing the Minefield: Establishing Safe Passage Through the Sensory Chaos of Autistic Spectrum Disorder*. Brighton: Pavilion.

Caldwell, P. (2005) *Finding You Finding Me: Using Intensive Interaction to Get in Touch with People whose Severe Learning Disabilities are Combined with Autistic Spectrum Disorder*. London: Jessica Kingsley Publishers.

Caldwell, P. (2007) *Inspirations – Reaching Ricky.* Available online at www.teachers.tv/video/13817. Accessed 6 December 2007. (Training video.)

Caldwell, P. with Horwood, J. (2007) *From Isolation to Intimacy: Making Friends without Words.* London: Jessica Kingsley Publishers.

Gillingham, G. (1995) *Autism: Handle with Care.* Arlington, TX: Future Horizons.

Happé, F., Ronald, A. and Plomin, R. (2006) 'Time to give up on a single explanation for autism.' *Nature Neuroscience 9*, 10, 1218–1220.

Horwood, J. (2004) *Activities to Promote Sensory Integration in Children.* Pamphlet available from: Caverstede Early Years Centre, Caverstede Rd, Walton, Peterborough PE4 6EX, UK (£2.50).

Horwood, J. (2006) *How to Become a Sensory Detective.* Pamphlet available from: Caverstede Early Years Centre, Caverstede Rd, Walton, Peterborough PE4 6EX, UK (£2.50).

Nind, M. and Hewett, D. (2001) *A Practical Guide to Intensive Interaction.* Kidderminster: British Institute of Learning Disabilities.

Ramachandran, V.S. (2006) 'Broken mirrors: A theory of autism.' *Scientific American Special Issue Neuroscience 295*, 5, 39–45.

BY PEOPLE WITH AUTISM

Blackburn, R. (2004) Flint NAS Seminar.

Gerland, G. (1996) *A Real Person.* London: Souvenir Press.

Grandin, T. in Arnall, D. and Peters, J. (1992) *A is for Autism.* London: A Finetake Production for BBC Radio 4.

Jolliffe, T., Lansdown, R. and Robinson, C. (1992) 'Autism: A personal account.' *Communication 26*, 3.

Lawson, W. (2003) *Build Your Own Life.* London: Jessica Kingsley Publishers.

Nazeer, K. (2006) *Send in the Idiots.* London: Bloomsbury Publishing.

Weekes, L. (date unknown) in *A Bridge of Voices.* Documentary of children talking about their experience of autism, BBC Radio 4.

Williams, D. (1992) *Somebody Somewhere.* London: Doubleday.

Williams, D. (1995) *Jam-Jar.* Channel 4 programme. Glasgow: Fresh Film and Television.

Williams, D. (1996) *Autism: An Inside-Out Approach.* London: Jessica Kingsley Publishers.

Williams, D. (1998) *Like Colour to the Blind: Soul Searching and Soul Finding.* London: Jessica Kingsley Publishers.

Williams, D. (1999) *Nobody Nowhere: The Remarkable Autobiography of an Autistic Girl.* London: Jessica Kingsley Publishers.

CONTACT INFORMATION FOR IRLEN LENSES IN THE UK

Irlen Lens Centre
4 Park Farm Business Centre
Fornham St Genevieve
Bury St Edmunds
Suffolk IP28 6TS
Tel. 01284 724301

About the Authors

Phoebe Caldwell is a practitioner who has been working with people with severe autism for 30 years. Originally a biologist, at first she was employed in the occupational therapy departments of a number of big hospitals. Since these closed she has worked freelance, employed by social services, health services, community providers, parent groups and individuals – wherever there was difficulty in getting touch with people with autism. She has worked mainly with those who are non-verbal but also with some who have speech and are more able. For four years she held a Joseph Rowntree Fellowship. Her supervisor was Geraint Ephraim, the psychologist who introduced a way of working with people which relies on using an individual's own body language to make contact with them. This approach is now known as Intensive Interaction, and is being used in many countries across the world. A dialogue develops during this approach, claiming the attention of both autistic and non-autistic partners. The aim is to establish emotional engagement, improving the ability to relate.

Jane Horwood is a paediatric occupational therapist with a special interest in the use of an approach known as Sensory Integration.[1] Sensory Integration helps people whose brains are unable to deal with the stimuli

---

1   Sensory Integration Theory was developed by Dr A. Jean Ayres in the 1950s. However, her work really became widely known when her book, *Sensory Integration and the Child*, was published in 1979.

they get from the world outside. It looks at the manner in which the brain organises all the sensory signals it receives, both those that tell it about the condition of the body itself and also the environment around it. Sound Sensory Integration helps provide meaning to what is experienced. When working with children on the autistic spectrum, Jane's aim is to introduce sensory interventions that are both meaningful and pleasurable for a particular child. She uses a variety of strong sensory signals to help children get a sense of where they are and what is going on round them.

Index